The *Gault* Case and Young People's Rights

Debating Supreme Court Decisions

Laura Cohen

D1737759

Enslow Publishers, Inc.
40 Industrial Road
Box 398
Berkeley Heights, NJ 07922
USA

http://www.enslow.com

105170

For my children, Adam and Claire Sullivan,
whose love of books inspired me to write one.

Library of Congress Cataloging-in-Publication Data

Cohen, Laura.
    The Gault case and young people's rights : debating Supreme Court decisions /
Laura Cohen.
        p. cm.—(Debating Supreme Court decisions)
    Includes bibliographical references and index.
    ISBN 0-7660-2476-8
    1. Gault, Gerald Francis, 1949 or 50—Trials, litigation, etc.—Juvenile literature.
2. Juvenile justice, Administration of—United States—Juvenile literature. 3. Due
process of law—United States—Juvenile literature. 4. Children—Legal status, laws,
etc.—United States—Juvenile literature. [1. Gault, Gerald Francis, 1949 or 50—Trials,
litigation, etc. 2. Justice, Administration of. 3. Children's rights. 4. Due process of law.
5. Juvenile courts.] I. Title. II. Series.
    KF228.G377C64 2006
    345.73'08—dc22

                                                                        2006001741
Printed in the United States of America

10 9 8 7 6 5 4 3 2 1

To Our Readers: We have done our best to make sure that all Internet Addresses in this
book were active and appropriate when we went to press. However, the author and publisher
have no control over and assume no liability for the material available on those Internet sites
or on other Web sites they may link to. Any comments or suggestions can be sent by e-mail
to comments@enslow.com or to the address on the back cover.

Illustration Credits: : Courtesy of the Arizona Historical Society/Tucson, AHS
#1000, p. 61; Fabian Bachrach/Collection of the Supreme Court of the United
States, p. 68; Bettmann/CORBIS, p. 9; courtesy of Norman Dorsen, p. 47; Hemera
Image Express, p. 2; Hessler Studios/Collection of the Supreme Court of the
United States, p. 35; Library of Congress, p. 18; National Geographic Society/
Collection of the Supreme Court of the United States, p. 79; photo courtesy of
Patricia Puritz/National Juvenile Defender Center, p. 95.

Cover Illustration: Artville (background); Shutterstock.com (photograph).

Contents

Acknowledgments

I am grateful to Norman Dorsen, Frederick I. and Grace A. Stokes Professor of Law and Counselor to the President at New York University, for generously sharing his memories of and reflections on the *Gault* case; to Patricia Puritz, Executive Director of the National Juvenile Defender Center, for her wonderful photograph of Gerald Gault and Amelia Lewis and for her steadfast commitment to building a juvenile defense bar that lives up to the promise of *In re Gault*; and to Michael Sullivan, without whom neither this book nor much else would be possible.

chapter 1

The Telephone Call

The morning of June 8, 1964, dawned hot and sunny in Globe, Arizona, a small town seventy-five miles east of Phoenix. Fifteen-year-old Gerald Gault and his friend, Ronald Lewis, had recently begun their summer vacation, and were "hanging out" at the Gault family's mobile home. Perhaps out of boredom, they made several prank telephone calls, during which one or both of the boys made rude remarks to a neighbor, Mrs. Cook. Gerald could not have known, when he put down the receiver that day, that his actions would reverberate far beyond Globe, reaching the United States Supreme Court and, ultimately, every juvenile court in the land.

A slight, dark-haired boy, Gerald had previously had two minor scrapes with the law. When he was thirteen, another boy accused Gerald of stealing a baseball glove, but the charge was dismissed. Two years later, in February 1964, the police found Gerald in the company of a boy who allegedly had stolen a wallet. As a result of this encounter, Gerald was brought before the Gila County Juvenile Court, which ordered him to "stay out of trouble" and placed him on probation for six months.[1] When a young person is placed on probation, he or she must report regularly to a probation officer. Usually, the probation officer makes sure that the young person is attending school, behaving at home, and staying out of trouble. In June 1964, a probation officer was still supervising Gerald Gault.

At around 10:00 A.M. on June 8, 1964, a Gila County Sheriff's officer knocked on the door of the Gault family home, arrested Gerald and Ronald, and took them to the Gila County Children's Detention Home. The detention home was a locked facility used to house children awaiting trial in family court. (Family courts, which are sometimes also called "children's courts," have the power to decide questions about child custody, child abuse and neglect, adoption, and juvenile delinquency.) Paul Gault, Gerald's father, was working near the Grand Canyon, miles away. Marjorie Gault, Gerald's mother, was at work in Globe, but no one called to tell her that her son had been arrested.

In fact, the deputy did not leave a formal notice or even a note informing her of Gerald's whereabouts.

Mrs. Gault returned home from work at 6:00 P.M. and found Gerald gone. Worried, she sent Gerald's older brother over to the Lewises' trailer to look for him. Only then did she learn what had happened to her son.

Fortunately, Mrs. Gault knew where the detention home was located, and she immediately went to find Gerald. Once inside, she encountered Charles Flagg, who was both the detention home's warden and a Gila County probation officer. Flagg would become a pivotal figure in the fate of Gerald Gault. He would not allow Mrs. Gault to see her son, but did explain why Gerald was there. He also told her that a hearing would be held in the local juvenile court at 3:00 P.M. the next day. Disheartened, Mrs. Gault went back to the family's trailer alone.

The First Hearing

The next day, Mrs. Gault attended the Family Court hearing with her older son; Gerald's father was still out of town, working. Also in the courtroom were Gerald, Officer Flagg, and Judge Robert McGhee. The Arizona Juvenile Code, which had been enacted a mere nine years earlier, made clear that probation officers were required to safeguard the interests of young people who were charged, as Gerald was, with juvenile delinquency. They also acted as prosecutors, presenting the charges to the court. In his role of prosecutor, Officer Flagg had filed a petition (legal document) asking Judge McGhee to decide whether Gerald should remain in his parents' custody or be sent to the State Training School, which was akin to a prison for young people.

The petition that Officer Flagg filed was not specific. It did not state what Gerald allegedly had said to Mrs. Cook or what law he allegedly broke. Nor did Gerald or his parents receive a copy of the petition until long after the juvenile court case was closed. As a result, when Gerald found himself in Judge McGhee's chambers on June 9, he still did not know precisely what he was accused of doing, what the possible punishment was, or what would happen at the hearing. More importantly, he had no lawyer to represent him.

Although Gerald was at risk of being sent to the training school until his twenty-first birthday, the hearing bore little resemblance to a typical criminal trial. Mrs. Cook, who made the complaint, was never required to come to court. Thus, Gerald could not confront her directly or cross-examine her. Instead, Officer Flagg told the judge what Mrs. Cook had said to him and what Gerald had told him about the incident. Testimony about statements made outside of the courtroom is called "hearsay" and is not permitted at most American trials. In this case, Officer Flagg's testimony about Mrs. Cook's version of the events was particularly unreliable, since it was based on a single telephone conversation between the two earlier that day.

In addition, it is difficult even now to know exactly what happened on June 9 because no transcript, which is a written or electronic record of a court proceeding, was made of the hearing.

This staged photo from 1946 simulates a situation like Gerald Gault's: The boy, who has been charged with juvenile delinquency, appears in front of the judge with his parents, but no attorney to protect his rights.

Transcripts are very important because they are the basis for appeals to higher courts. Without a transcript, an appeals court cannot know exactly what happened in the lower court or what mistakes might have been made.

Although those who were present on June 9 all testified at a later hearing that Judge McGhee questioned Gerald about the telephone call, they did not agree on what Gerald said in response to those questions. According to Mrs. Gault, Gerald only admitted dialing the neighbor's telephone number and then handing the telephone to Ronald Lewis. Officer Flagg, on the other hand, remembered that Gerald had admitted making all of the offensive comments. Judge McGhee had yet a third recollection, testifying that Gerald confessed to making one of the remarks.[2] The legal term for the type of remark was *lewd*, which means "vulgar, obscene." Thus, even with regard to the central question of the case—did Gerald in fact break the law by making an offensive telephone call?—no record exists of precisely what was said in the juvenile court.

At the end of the June 9 hearing, Gerald was sent back to the detention center for three more days. He finally was released to his parents on either Thursday, June 11, or Friday, June 12. (The lack of a record led to confusion about this seemingly simple fact, too; Officer Flagg recalled that

Gerald was released on June 11, but his mother was sure it was June 12.) At 5:00 P.M. on the day of his release, Mrs. Gault received a brief, undated, handwritten note from Officer Flagg, informing her that Judge McGhee had scheduled "further Hearings on Gerald's delinquency" for the following Monday, June 15.[3]

Return to Court

On Monday morning, Gerald and his parents returned to the courthouse. Once again, Judge McGhee questioned Gerald about the telephone call; once again, because there was no transcript, those present later differed on what Gerald actually said. Mrs. Gault, grasping one of the fundamental flaws of the process, asked that Mrs. Cook be forced to appear in court. Judge McGhee refused her request.

During this court session, the probation officers (Flagg and Henderson) submitted a report about Gerald and his family to Judge McGhee. Neither Gerald nor his parents received a copy of the report, even though it formed the basis for Judge McGhee's ultimate decision in the case.[4]

Gerald Gault's Sentence

At the conclusion of the June 15 hearing, the worst fears of the Gault family were realized. Based on what he termed "full hearing and due deliberation," Judge McGhee found fifteen-year-old Gerald to be a "delinquent child" based upon the offense of "Lewd Phone Calls," and committed him to the Arizona State Industrial School until his twenty-first birthday.[5] By contrast, an adult found guilty of the same offense could have been sentenced to a maximum jail term of two months and a fine of fifty dollars.[6]

Although he received a much harsher sentence than an adult would have faced, Gerald was denied the protections that form the core of the due process of law guaranteed by the United States Constitution. Had he been an adult, Gerald would have received written notice of the charges against him, outlining the facts upon which those charges were based. He would have had the right to a trial that was not based on hearsay evidence, in which Mrs. Cook would be called to testify, and the right to cross-examine her and any other witnesses. He would have been protected by the "privilege against self-incrimination," meaning that Judge McGhee could not have forced him to testify if he did not wish to do so. And, perhaps most importantly, he would have had the right to a defense lawyer, even if he could not afford to pay.

Years later, Gerald Gault acknowledged the devastating impact that the lack of legal representation had on him and the outcome of his case. Because he did not have a lawyer to explain the proceedings to him, to challenge the evidence, and to argue on his behalf, he did not understand what was happening to him. It was not until Judge McGhee uttered the words "committed until he was twenty-one," and Gerald "realized that was more years than he could count on the fingers of one hand,"[7] that reality began to sink in.

Gerald was sent to Fort Grant, a century-old army barracks located 90 miles from Globe.[8] He ultimately spent six months in this decrepit facility. His heartbroken parents, although they had little money, were determined to right the injustice they believed had been inflicted on themselves and their son. Little did they know, when they left the Gila County courthouse that day, that their quest would take them to the United States Supreme Court and would shake the very foundation of America's juvenile justice system.

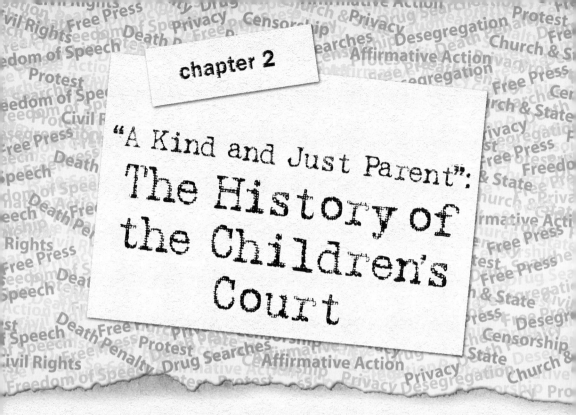

chapter 2

"A Kind and Just Parent": The History of the Children's Court

Why did Judge McGhee handle the case against Gerald Gault in such an informal manner? Why were the hearings held privately in the judge's chambers rather than a public courtroom, without lawyers or a court reporter? Why did Gerald receive a six-year term of incarceration, rather than the relatively mild sentence Judge McGhee could have imposed if he were an adult? The answers to these questions lie in the nature of the juvenile justice system of the time.

America's juvenile courts in 1963 were the result of a reform movement that had begun nearly seventy years earlier in Chicago. Before the nineteenth century, children over the age of seven who were convicted of crimes, including minor offenses like shoplifting, were sent to adult prisons. There, conditions were harsh. Children often were abused by other inmates and guards, malnourished, and forced to perform hard labor. Some children also were sentenced to death, including death by public hanging.[1]

In the 1820s, reformers who believed that most juvenile crime was the result of poverty, neglect, and the disorder of city life created "houses of refuge," where children thought to be at risk of criminal behavior were sent to live, away from their families. By the late nineteenth century, however, concerns about abuse inside these institutions led to the closing of most houses of refuge.

From 1850 to 1900, American society underwent dramatic changes as immigration increased and large numbers of people moved from rural areas to cities. There, they encountered the problems that still exist today: poverty, housing shortages, crowding, poor hygiene, unemployment, and crime. As a result, more children were neglected and more were caught up in the criminal justice system.

In Chicago, where conditions were among the worst in the country, a young woman named Jane Addams decided to take action. She took over a crumbling old mansion in one of the city's poorest neighborhoods and created Hull House, the first settlement house in the nation. Young, college-educated men and women who wanted to help the poor came to live and work at Hull House. They reached out to the children and families in the surrounding neighborhoods, trying to enrich the lives of people who had little money or education.

Addressing Youth Crime

Through her daily contact with her less fortunate neighbors, Addams saw many children who were accused of thefts and other wrongdoing. She soon came to believe that society's response to youth crime, and the mixing of children and adults in the criminal justice system, caused more harm than good. In fact, it seemed that instead of teaching them a lesson, incarcerating young people in adult jails and prisons led them to commit more crimes. Similarly, because much juvenile crime went completely unpunished, many children did not receive any form of help or intervention until it was too late.

Addams and her colleague, Julia Lathrop, led a campaign to establish a separate justice system for juveniles. Their aim was to create a true alternative to criminal prosecution of children. The primary goal was rehabilitation—the treatment of the problems that led children to misbehave in the first place. Children were not to be considered criminals; instead, Addams and Lathrop coined the term "juvenile delinquency," which covered a wide range of behavior that might indicate a need for some type of treatment or help for the child and his or her family. Because the court was intended to protect children rather than punish them, the definition of delinquency included not only crimes but also such activities as running away, associating with "undesirable companions," truancy from school, and—as Gerald Gault came to learn six decades later—using inappropriate language.[2]

Judges and politicians soon embraced this new approach to addressing youthful misbehavior. Judge Julian Mack, the first juvenile court judge in Chicago, wrote that the primary question for the juvenile court was not "Has this boy or girl committed a specific wrong, but What is he, how has he become what he is, and what had best be done in his interest and in the interest of the state to save him from a downward career?" Judge Mack also wrote that it was important for children to feel that judges cared about them and paid attention to their needs.[3]

Central to the new juvenile court was the idea that the court system (and, in fact, government as a whole) should have the same responsibilities to care for, nurture, and protect young people as their parents. This idea is called *parens patriae*, or "state as

Jane Addams was one of the reformers who saw a need to change the way of dealing with children who had been charged with crimes. She led a movement to establish a separate justice system for juveniles.

parent." Because the new court was to act as "a kind and just parent," furthermore, its founders believed that children did not need lawyers, and the rules governing what could be said or done during court were relaxed. The words used to describe what happened in court were also different. Children were called "respondents" rather than defendants. They received a "disposition" instead of a sentence, and, rather than being "convicted," they were "adjudicated delinquent."

The juvenile court was different in other significant ways, as well. With the memory of British "star chambers"—secret courts that dealt out harsh punishments—still fresh in their minds, the authors of the United States Constitution insisted on a court system that was open to the public and the press. As a result, American courts had always been accessible to anyone who wanted to attend. However, the founders of the juvenile court were afraid that bad publicity might destroy children's chances for rehabilitation, which led them to insist on closed, private proceedings.

The Illinois Juvenile Court Act, which was enacted in 1899 and served as the basis for juvenile court laws across the country, was based on three central concerns: (1) the protection and development of children; (2) the protection of society; and (3) the protection of the family. Because judges were required to balance these three, often competing, interests, they were given a great deal of flexibility to tailor their actions to each individual child. Unlike adult sentencing laws, which specify ranges of punishment for different categories of crimes, the new juvenile code permitted judges to send young people home to their families with supervision or treatment, place them on probation, or place them in foster care. In fact, because one of the aims of the court was the preservation of the family, children were to be incarcerated only as a last resort.

The idea of the juvenile court caught on quickly and soon spread to every state. As Judge Ben Lindsey of the Denver Juvenile Court stated, "The criminal court for child-offenders is based on the doctrine of fear, degradation and punishment. It was, and is, absurd. The Juvenile Court was founded on the principle of love."[4]

Problems in the Juvenile Justice System

Unfortunately, as early as the 1920s, some legal scholars began to doubt that the informal approach to juvenile justice was effective. With informality came broad powers, or discretion, for judges. Although many juvenile court judges were well-meaning, they did not all share the same opinions as Jane Addams and the other reformers about what was best for children, or even agree that children should remain in their parents' custody whenever possible. Young people like Gerald Gault were often sent to state training schools and juvenile institutions for many years on the basis of minor offenses, without the benefit of lawyers or real trials.

Conditions in those institutions often were terrible; they were run-down, had inadequate schools and treatment programs, and did little to prepare children for life after release. As a result, children who came before the juvenile court and were sent to training schools often committed new crimes, and it became increasingly clear that the goals of "treatment, training, and rehabilitation" were not being met.[5]

In addition, because children in most states could not appeal juvenile court decisions, there was nothing that they or their parents (whose parental rights were undermined when their children were placed involuntarily in state custody) could do to challenge a court ruling. As a result, legal scholars began to question whether *parents* of children caught up in the system were being denied due process; few yet recognized that the children themselves might enjoy constitutional protections.

By the 1950s, furthermore, public concern about juvenile crime was swelling. Throughout the decade, the number of juvenile arrests grew dramatically.[6] As fears about youth crime grew, so did fears that the informal, rehabilitative juvenile court was no longer effective. An outcry arose in many states for more formal court procedures, and legislatures began to change their juvenile laws. By the time Gerald Gault's case made its way to the United States Supreme Court, a fundamental transformation of the juvenile court system had already begun.

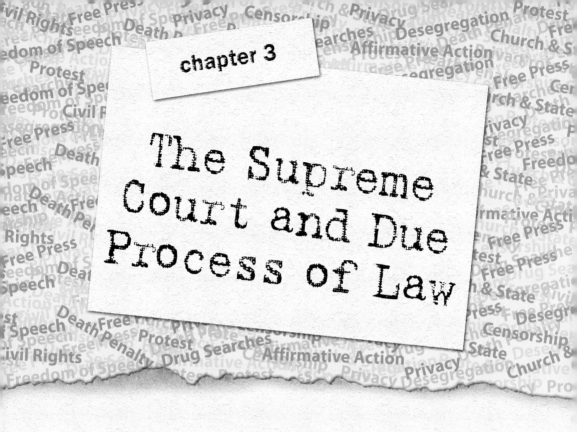

chapter 3

The Supreme Court and Due Process of Law

Why, in 1964—175 years after the birth of the United States Constitution—was it not perfectly clear whether Gerald Gault had the right to a lawyer, or to remain silent, or to cross-examine Mrs. Cook? And, if young people did have these rights, how could they have gone unrecognized since the creation of the nation's first juvenile court, sixty-five years earlier?

The answers to these questions lie at the heart of the American legal system and the complicated relationship among the three branches of government. Most of the personal rights and liberties that we consider to be central to citizenship—freedom of speech, freedom of religion, and the rights of criminal defendants, to name a few—are found in the Bill of Rights, the first ten amendments to the United States Constitution. Although the Constitution is the ultimate law of the land, most of the rules that govern our society are found in statutes, or laws, passed either by Congress or by state legislatures. Usually, statutes do not conflict with the Constitution and there is no need to challenge them.

Sometimes, however, a statute may violate a constitutional right. For example, the Arizona Juvenile Code, which controlled the way the juvenile court ran in Arizona, did not state that children charged with delinquency had the right to a lawyer. Yet the Sixth Amendment of the Constitution states that "in all criminal prosecutions, the accused shall enjoy the right . . . to have the assistance of counsel for his defence." Was a juvenile delinquency prosecution considered a "criminal prosecution?" What is the "assistance of counsel?" If a child could not afford to pay for a lawyer, could the Sixth Amendment be read to mean that the government would have to provide one? And, who is responsible for deciding the answers to these questions?

Challenging the Laws

When a statute (such as the Arizona Juvenile Code) appears to violate the Constitution, a person who is harmed by that statute (such as Gerald Gault) may challenge it in the courts. Similarly, one may challenge actions taken by a governmental employee or agency (such as Officer Flagg) or decisions made by a judge (such as Judge McGhee) that appear to violate the Constitution. It is then up to the courts to interpret the meaning of the constitutional section involved and decide whether the law or action in question was unconstitutional. Often, this is a multistep process, beginning in the lowest level trial court and ending either in a state supreme court or the United States Supreme Court.

Another question that had not been answered fully by the time Judge McGhee sent Gerald Gault to Fort Grant was whether the Bill of Rights protected people from actions taken by state governments at all. When the Bill of Rights was adopted in 1791, it was understood only to prevent abuses by the *federal* government; the states were free to treat their citizens as they saw fit. At the end of the Civil War, however, Congress recognized that newly freed slaves needed to be recognized as citizens and to be protected from maltreatment by the southern states. In 1868, the Fourteenth Amendment to the Constitution was adopted, which says, in part: "No State may deprive any person of life, liberty, or property without due process of law."

Like other sections of the Constitution, it was left to the United States Supreme Court to determine whether the provisions of the Bill of Rights would apply to state governments. The question the Court began asking in the 1920s was whether the particular right involved—freedom of speech or freedom of religion, for example—is essential to a fundamentally fair legal system. If so, the right or freedom in question is part of due process, and state governments must protect and uphold it.

In the early 1960s, just before Gerald Gault began to make his way through the court system, the Supreme Court decided a series of criminal cases that applied other parts of the Bill of Rights to the states. In *Mapp* v. *Ohio*, the Court held that state police and other officials were bound by Fourth Amendment guarantee of freedom from unlawful searches, and that evidence obtained in violation of that right could not be used in court.[1] Two years later, in *Gideon* v. *Wainwright*, the Court found that the Sixth Amendment required states to pay for lawyers for poor defendants in felony cases.[2] The Court also held that due process included the right to confront and cross-examine witnesses[3] and the privilege against self-incrimination,[4] which protects defendants from being forced to speak to the police or testify in court. Finally, in the case of *Miranda* v. *Arizona*, the Court held that due process required police officers to warn criminal suspects of their right to remain silent and their right to counsel before questioning them.[5]

Rights for Young People

All of these decisions, of course, involved adults. Children, on the other hand, did not—and still do not—have many of the rights adults enjoy. They cannot vote, enter into contracts, or make certain decisions without the consent of their parents or guardians. It thus was not clear whether the Supreme Court, if asked to do so, would extend any of the recently recognized due process rights to delinquency proceedings, in spite of the growing concern about the shortcomings of the nation's juvenile courts.

In 1966, however, a strong signal went out. In *Kent v. United States*, the Court found that young people who could be tried as adults due to the serious nature of the charges against them had a right to a lawyer and other protections when the juvenile court considered transferring them to the adult system.[6] Although the case did not deal specifically with the question of whether children involved in delinquency proceedings were entitled to these safeguards, the Court observed:

> There is much evidence that some juvenile courts . . . lack the personnel, facilities and techniques to perform adequately as representatives of the State . . . at least with respect to children charged with law violation. There is some evidence, in fact, that there

may be grounds for concern that the child receives the worst of both worlds: that he gets neither the protections accorded to adults nor the solicitous care and . . . treatment [needed by] children.[7]

With these words, the stage was set. It was time for Gerald Gault to enter the scene.

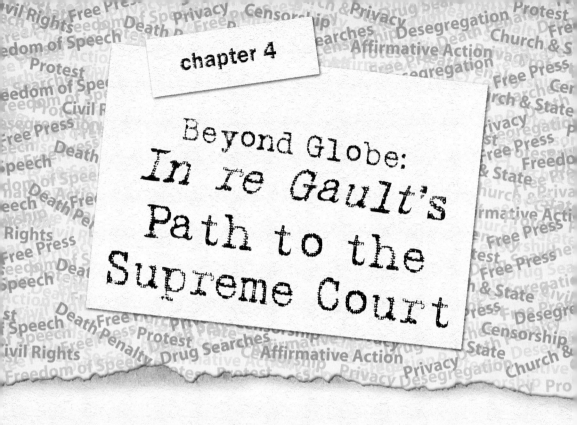

chapter 4

Beyond Globe: In re Gault's Path to the Supreme Court

Marjorie and Paul Gault left Judge McGhee's courtroom on June 15, 1964, badly shaken. That they lost custody of their son so quickly, without any real opportunity to defend him or themselves, was stunning. The Gaults were determined to obtain Gerald's release from the training school.

Great legal victories in the United States are often partly a matter of chance, the meeting of the right lawyer with the right client at the right time. The *Gault* case was no exception. Six weeks after Judge McGhee issued his order, the Gaults were referred to Amelia Lewis, an experienced attorney who had moved to Arizona from New York several years earlier. Lewis was a volunteer lawyer for the Arizona chapter of the American Civil Liberties

Union (ACLU), an organization dedicated to protecting and defending constitutional rights in the United States. She met with Mr. and Mrs. Gault on August 1, and, although she had no prior experience with juvenile delinquency matters, she agreed to take the case.[1]

The first question confronting Lewis was what legal mechanism would permit her to bring Gerald's case before a higher court. In most situations, a person who is unhappy with a lower court's decision can appeal the matter to the next level of the judicial system, generally called an appeals court. Depending on the nature of the case, two or three appeals may be made, ending in either the highest court in the state (generally the state supreme court) or the United States Supreme Court.

Appellate courts generally focus on whether the trial court made a mistake, either in the way it conducted the trial or in the way it applied the law to the facts of the case. Unlike a trial court, appellate courts do not hear testimony of witnesses or consider any new evidence. Instead, their decisions are based on review of the transcripts, or records, of the lower court and on legal arguments made by lawyers for the people on each side of the dispute. Lawyers submit briefs, or written arguments, to the appellate court and also make presentations to the court in person. This is known as oral argument.

In 1964, however, Arizona's Juvenile Code did not require the Family Court to make a transcript of juvenile delinquency proceedings and did not permit children to appeal a Family Court judge's decision. Thus, no written record of what took place in Judge McGhee's courtroom existed, and Lewis was not permitted to appeal Gerald's incarceration. Instead, she filed a petition for a writ of habeas corpus in the Arizona Supreme Court on August 3, 1964. The Supreme Court then referred the matter to the Maricopa County Superior Court, a lower level court in Phoenix.[2]

The Right to Due Process

The writ of habeas corpus is one of the central rights guaranteed to citizens under the United States Constitution. Translated from the Latin, it means "you have the body," and it is a method for challenging an unlawful imprisonment. In light of England's history of arbitrarily incarcerating citizens who were believed to be disloyal to the king, the authors of the Constitution ensured that the writ of habeas corpus was embedded in American law. A court hearing a habeas corpus petition does not consider whether the incarcerated person is guilty or innocent; instead, the only question before it is whether the person was

Legal Terms

appellant or petitioner—The person who feels the lower court made an error.

appellate court (also called court of appeals)—A court that reviews decisions of lower courts for fairness and accuracy. An appellate court can reverse a lower court's ruling.

appellee or respondent—The person who won the case in the lower court.

brief—Written statement of a party's argument on one or more issues in the case.

concur—To agree with the majority in a court case.

dissent—To disagree with the majority in a court case.

majority opinion—The ruling and reasoning supported by a majority of appellate court judges in a case. **Concurring opinions** are written by judges who agree with the majority opinion but have other reasons for their views. **Dissenting opinions** are written by judges who disagree with the ruling.

oral argument—The process by which lawyers present legal arguments in person to a court, especially an appeals court.

precedent—A legal holding that will determine how courts decide future cases.

denied due process by the trial court and, so, is imprisoned unlawfully.

American courts up until this point had paid little attention to due process rights for children, but had long recognized the rights of parents to raise their own children. Thus, when Lewis filed her petition, she asserted that because Gerald's *parents* had not received adequate notice of the charges against Gerald and the hearings, and because they did not have the right to legal counsel, they were unlawfully deprived of custody of their son. Consequently, the state of Arizona was holding him illegally.[3]

The Maricopa County Superior Court judge, Fred Hyder, scheduled a hearing on the habeas corpus petition for August 17. For the first time, a transcript was made of testimony relating to Gerald Gault's incarceration at Fort Grant. Although Judge McGhee, Officer Flagg, and Mr. and Mrs. Gault all testified at the August 17 hearing, they disagreed significantly about precisely what had been said at Gerald's delinquency trial a mere two months earlier, underscoring the importance of an accurate record of court proceedings.[4]

Trial court judges do not testify at appellate arguments, and generally do not testify at habeas corpus hearings. Because no transcript existed of the June proceedings, however, the Superior Court was forced to take testimony from Judge McGhee. When asked what the basis was for his finding of juvenile delinquency, Judge McGhee could not recall precisely. As the United States Supreme Court later noted:

> At the habeas corpus hearing on August 17, Judge McGhee was vigorously cross-examined as to the basis for his actions. He testified that he had taken into account the fact that Gerald was on proba- tion. . . . Asked about the basis for his conclusion that Gerald was "habitually involved in immoral mat- ters," the judge testified, somewhat vaguely, that two years earlier . . . a "referral" was made concerning Gerald "where the boy had stolen a baseball glove from another boy and lied to the Police Department about it." The judge said there was "no hearing" and "no accusation" relating to this incident, "because of lack of material foundation." But it seems to have remained in his mind as a relevant factor.[5]

Despite this murky testimony, Judge Hyder quickly denied the writ of habeas corpus. Lewis's next step was an appeal to the Arizona Supreme Court. At this point, after discussions with other Arizona ACLU lawyers, she significantly revised her legal strategy. Rather than focusing solely on Judge McGhee's failure to follow the requirements of the Juvenile Code and failure to tell the Gaults of their right to counsel, she made six separate arguments challenging the constitutionality of the Juvenile Code itself, the way the juvenile court had con- ducted the delinquency hearing, and the conduct of the habeas proceeding. In addition to those made earlier, these arguments included challenges to the Family Court's refusal to permit the Gaults to confront Mrs. Cook, Gerald's accuser; Judge McGhee's decision to force Gerald to testify; and the court's failure to state the factual reasons for its determination that Gerald was delinquent. For the first time, Lewis also argued that in order to find a child delinquent, the court should require proof "beyond a reasonable doubt."[6] Finally, she argued that the failure of the Juvenile Code to provide for transcripts and appeals in delinquency cases was a violation of due process.

Although it would seem, with hindsight, that these arguments would best support Gerald's own right to be free from unlawful imprisonment, Lewis clung to her theory that it was Paul and Marjorie Gault, rather than their son, whose rights had been violated. The American judicial system is rooted in the concept of legal precedent, a process in which courts consider how higher courts have decided similar issues and, to a great extent, are required to follow those prior decisions. This is particularly true of constitutional questions, because the United States Supreme Court is the ultimate interpreter of the Constitution and because rights that are not explicitly recognized by the specific words of the

Constitution itself are carved out hesitantly, slowly, and carefully.

The Rights of Parents

In 1964, the notion of parental rights was firmly ensconced in American law. Both the United States Supreme Court and the Arizona Supreme Court had recognized that parents have a clear right to custody of their own children, as long as it has not been legally determined that they have been neglectful or abusive. Moreover, the Arizona Supreme

These are the justices of the Supreme Court who would ultimately decide the Gault case. It was known as the Warren court because of the Chief Justice, Earl Warren (center front).

Court had found, a mere eight years earlier, that parents who were threatened with the removal of their children by child welfare officials had a right to due process in the Family Court.[7] Thus, Lewis argued that unless the state could prove in court that Gerald's delinquent activity *resulted from* neglect by his parents, there was no legal basis for depriving them of custody. In addition, she asserted that if the government wishes to deprive parents of custody involuntarily, whether on the basis of parental neglect or on delinquent activity by the child, the parents must be accorded the fundamental due process rights outlined in her brief.[8]

The state of Arizona vigorously opposed the Gaults' appeal, and the Arizona Supreme Court ultimately rejected her arguments. Although it agreed that children and their parents enjoyed due process rights in juvenile delinquency proceedings, it continued to embrace the notion that relaxed standards were acceptable and consistent with the Family Court's *parens patriae* obligations. The court determined that notice of the charges and opportunity to prepare for a hearing were required, but that Gerald and his parents had in fact received sufficient notice and time. It found that delinquency charges must be proven by "clear and convincing evidence," which is less than the "beyond a reasonable doubt" level of proof proposed by Lewis. Finally, the court rejected Lewis's assertion that due process required transcripts of delinquency proceedings and the right of appeal.[9]

In all, the decision was a resounding defeat for Amelia Lewis as well as Gerald Gault and his family. One glimmer of hope came through the court's opinion, however. Although Lewis did not make this argument, the court acknowledged that children had a stake in the outcome of juvenile delinquency proceedings that was separate and apart from that of their parents and, so, enjoyed distinct due process rights in the juvenile court: "Good intentions do not justify depriving a child of due process of law. . . . Fairness is not inimical [opposed] to the proper treatment of juveniles."[10] With this subtle nod to the individual rights of young people, the door to the United States Supreme Court swung open.

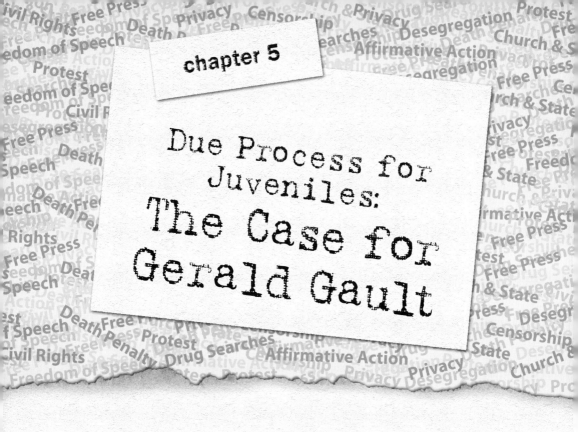

chapter 5

Due Process for Juveniles: The Case for Gerald Gault

After the Arizona Supreme Court refused to release Gerald Gault, Amelia Lewis decided to look for help. She turned to a young New York University law professor, Norman Dorsen, who was forging a reputation as a champion of civil rights and civil liberties. Dorsen had been a classmate of Amelia Lewis's son at Columbia University in New York. He had served as law clerk to Supreme Court Justice John Marshall Harlan nine years earlier and, although he had never argued a case before the Court, he was well-versed in its workings.[1]

At the time he received the case file from Lewis, Dorsen was handling a number of appeals for the ACLU's national office; in fact, he later served as the organization's president for fifteen years. He was also busy writing a book and teaching. Forty years later, he recalled, "I initially didn't take the case as seriously as I should have."[2] He asked a colleague, Gertrude Mainzer, who specialized in social welfare law, to review Lewis's materials. Mainzer soon reported back that the case raised important issues and could bring about major changes in juvenile law.[3] It was then that Dorsen took a careful look and realized how potentially significant the case was.[4]

Once again, the Gault family benefited from a fortunate meeting of lawyer and case. The ACLU had been involved in many of the constitutional and criminal law cases that had been heard by the Supreme Court in recent years, and was willing to throw its considerable weight behind Dorsen's efforts. Dorsen also drew on the expertise of several colleagues, including Mainzer and Daniel Rezneck, a lawyer at the Arnold and Porter law firm in Washington, D.C., to help him shape the legal arguments and write the brief to the Supreme Court.[5]

A New Strategy

Dorsen began by abandoning the central points that Lewis had made in Arizona. He believed that the compelling facts of the *Gault* case did not lend themselves to an argument in favor of parents' rights but, instead, strongly supported the extension of due process rights to *children* charged with delinquency. Initially, Rezneck suggested that Dorsen focus on the right to counsel, since "all of this comes down to whether a person has a lawyer."[6] Ultimately, though, Dorsen decided otherwise. He included three other constitutional protections already extended to adults in criminal cases: the right to notice of charges and hearings, the right of confrontation and cross-examination, and the privilege against self-incrimination. In addition, he urged the Court to mandate the keeping of a transcript of juvenile court proceedings and to recognize the right to appeal from the juvenile court.

Dorsen's first task was to file a notice of appeal with the Supreme Court. Because the Court accepts fewer than one hundred cases each year, lawyers who are attempting to have their matters heard must first convince the justices that their cases raise important questions of constitutional or federal law. The notice of appeal thus carefully framed the question that the ACLU and the Gault family were asking the Court to consider:

> Whether the Juvenile Code of Arizona . . . on its face or as construed and applied, is invalid under the Due Process Clause of the Fourteenth Amendment to the [U.S.] Constitution because it authorizes a juvenile to be taken from the custody of his parents and to be committed to a state institution by a judicial proceeding which confers unlimited discretion upon the Juvenile Court.[7]

The notice then outlined the specific protections that were denied to Gerald Gault and other young people caught up in Arizona's juvenile court system.[8]

With Daniel Rezneck, Norman Dorsen next began drafting the legal brief that he would submit to the Supreme Court on behalf of Gerald and his parents. Its arguments and reasoning would become the backbone of the juvenile justice system in the years to come.

The Brief for Gault

The starting point for any legal argument is the facts of the case: What actually happened to the people involved? How were they affected by the actions of another person, the government, or a lower court? Were they harmed in some way? It is only through a clear retelling of the facts that lawyers can most effectively assert legal positions. Dorsen commented many years later, "I took enormous pains with the preparation of the facts, because these facts [what had happened to Gerald Gault] were so good that if they were set out with clarity and force it would take us a long way."[9]

He began by summarizing the events that had led Gerald from the Gila County Detention Home to Fort Grant to the United States Supreme Court. He focused on those details that would best support Gerald's constitutional claims, including

◇ the juvenile court's failure to provide either Gerald or his parents with written notice of the charges or hearing;

◇ Judge McGhee's refusal to require Mrs. Cook's presence in court and his failure to tell either Gerald or his parents of the right to counsel;

◇ Judge McGhee's questioning of Gerald without advising him of the privilege against self-incrimination; and

◇ the many gaps in information and factual inconsistencies that resulted from the juvenile court's failure to keep a record of the proceedings.

Dorsen drove this point home effectively when he wrote, "It is difficult, based on the Juvenile Judge's testimony, to know with certainty what the basis was for the finding of delinquency."[10]

Knowing that Justice Abe Fortas might well take the lead for the Court in deciding the case, Dorsen noted the "gap between ideal and reality"[11] by strategically quoting from Fortas's recent opinion in *Kent* v. *United States*:

> There is evidence, in fact, that there may be grounds for concern that the child receives the worst of both worlds: that he gets neither the protections accorded to adults nor the solicitous care and regenerative treatment postulated for children.[12]

Dorsen further asserted that the failure to provide children with due process could not be justified by what the brief termed the "mischievous notion that what is being meted out in juvenile proceedings is 'treatment,' and not 'punishment.'"[13] The supposed distinction between adult punishment and juvenile treatment evaporated when examined closely. In fact, delinquent children were often treated more harshly and suffered a greater loss of liberty than adults found guilty of identical offenses. Gerald Gault, for example, who technically could not be "punished," was committed to the training school at Fort Grant for up to six years for making a lewd telephone call, while an adult found guilty of the same offense could receive a maximum of only two months in the county jail. As a California court had noted fourteen years earlier, the notion that children were not subject to punishment was "a legal fiction presenting a challenge to credulity and doing violence to reason."[14]

Most of the brief was devoted to establishing that in granting juvenile court judges broad powers to treat children charged with delinquency as they saw fit, the Arizona Juvenile Code denied Gerald Gault and others like him the basic rights guaranteed by the United States Constitution.[15] Because the Supreme Court, when it considers expanding constitutional protections, will often look to what current practices are in different parts of the country, Dorsen pointed out that numerous state supreme courts, state statutes, legal scholars, and professional associations already recognized the importance of due process rights for children in the juvenile court.

The brief went on to target the six specific protections that were denied to Gerald Gault and to argue that these rights must be extended to children in juvenile delinquency cases. Four of these—notice, confrontation, counsel, and the privilege against self-incrimination—had already been recognized by the Court to be essential elements of due process for adult criminal defendants. The other two—transcript and appellate review—had not.

Notice of Charges and Hearing. Notice of the charges one is facing, and notice of when and where a hearing on those charges will be held, is the first, essential element of due process. A person charged with violating the law simply cannot defend him- or herself without knowing precisely what it is that he or she is accused of doing, what laws allegedly were violated, and when the trial will take place.

By the time the *Gault* case arrived at the Supreme Court in 1966, the right to notice was well-established for adults. Dorsen asserted that the Court should recognize a similar right to notice in juvenile delinquency cases. Since many children might not understand the notice, Dorsen argued that their parents must also receive notice.

That neither Gerald Gault nor his parents received adequate notice of either the charges or the delinquency hearing was clear. The only way that Mrs. Gault found out about the June 9 hearing was by going to the detention home on the night of June 8, when Officer Flagg told her to be in court the next day. The only written notice the Gaults ever received from anyone connected with the case was the handwritten note from Officer Flagg on Friday, June 12, telling them that "further hearings on Gerald's delinquency" would take place on Monday, June 15. Neither message gave the Gaults sufficient time or information to prepare a defense.

Gerald was placed at an even greater disadvantage by the failure of anyone, at any time, to inform him or his parents of the precise nature of the charges against him. Although a written petition, or legal document, was filed in court on June 9, it did not state that Gerald was accused of violating the obscene language section of the Arizona Criminal Code or that he was accused of an ongoing course of bad behavior. It did not state what Gerald was accused of saying to Mrs. Cook, or that he could be found to be delinquent based on the prior incident involving the baseball glove. As a result of this inadequate notice, the brief argued, Gerald was denied due process.

Right to Counsel. Recognition of the right to counsel in juvenile cases was one of Dorsen's and the ACLU's central goals, because none of the other elements of due process would have much meaning if children did not have lawyers to assist them. Most children (and, in fact, most adults) cannot understand the legal requirements of notice, cross-examine effectively, write appeals, or evaluate the pros and cons of testifying in court. Nor can a juvenile court judge, no matter how well-meaning, conduct necessary investigation, prepare witnesses to testify, or offer children the objective legal advice necessary to make the best decisions. Juvenile courts across the country, even in 1966, were often overwhelmed, and many of the judges were not even lawyers.

In addition to these "real world" factors, Dorsen relied on earlier cases and current practice in different parts of the country to drive the point home. The question was not only whether better-off families should be allowed to hire lawyers to represent their children but also, more importantly, whether the state should be required to provide defense lawyers for children who could not afford to hire one. In addition, it was critical to draw a distinction between the right of parents to hire counsel to protect their child custody rights

Norman Dorsen was a law professor who agreed to argue Gerald Gault's case before the Supreme Court. He is shown here many years after the Gault case.

(which was recognized by the Arizona Supreme Court in its opinion in the *Gault* matter) and an independent right of representation for children charged with delinquency.

The Supreme Court's prior decisions in the area of right to counsel in criminal cases had made clear that adults facing criminal charges in state courts enjoy a right to counsel and that a lawyer must be provided for defendants who cannot afford to hire one. There were several bases for these decisions. The Sixth Amendment to the United States Constitution guarantees the right of legal representation to people facing criminal charges in federal courts, and the Fourteenth Amendment's due process clause states that a person may not be deprived of "life, liberty, or property without due process of law." In order to establish the right to counsel in state criminal cases, the Court held in *Powell* v. *Alabama* that legal representation was an essential element of due process, and so was required by the Fourteenth Amendment.[16] In *Gideon* v. *Wainwright*, the Court went one step further and determined that the right to counsel was so fundamental that lawyers must be provided free of charge to criminal defendants who cannot afford to hire one.[17]

The question for the Court in *Gault*, then, was whether juvenile delinquency cases (which, because of the emphasis on treatment rather than punishment, are not technically considered "criminal") pose enough of a threat to a child's liberty to require due process and, consequently, the right to counsel. Not surprisingly, Dorsen answered this question with a resounding "yes" by looking at other, noncriminal matters in which the Court had recognized a right to legal representation. In *Kent* v. *United States*, for example, the Court found that children who were threatened with transfer from the juvenile to the adult criminal system enjoyed a right to counsel, since the decision to transfer would carry a significant threat to liberty.[18] Similarly, the Court had recognized the right of adults facing the threat of criminal charges to legal representation outside the courtroom; in *Miranda* v. *Arizona*, for instance, the Court held that suspects being questioned by the police have a right to have a lawyer present. They must be told of that right by police and agree to proceed without a lawyer before questioning can occur.[19]

As Gerald Gault's situation made clear, delinquency proceedings threatened a child's right to reside with his family, to go to his own school, and to live his life free from governmental supervision and control. Whether the case was technically "criminal" or not, being committed to a state-run institution for up to six years surely deprived children of their liberty.

Finally, many American legal writers, state courts, and modern juvenile laws had by 1966 acknowledged the critical importance of legal counsel to children charged with delinquency. The tide of legal thought was turning toward recognition of the right to counsel, and, Dorsen argued, the United States Supreme Court should follow suit.

Right of Confrontation and Cross-Examination. The ability to confront, or challenge, witnesses had long been considered central to the American judicial system. The right of confrontation involves two elements: (1) that the witness be present in court and required to testify about facts of which he or she has knowledge; and (2) that the opposing party, or that person's lawyer, be given an opportunity to *cross-examine* the witness.

Cross-examination is a form of questioning that is aimed at revealing inconsistencies, exposing untruths, and suggesting faults of logic in the witness's testimony. Although it is rarely as dramatic as television would have one believe, it requires great skill to be effective. It also is one of the most important elements of the trial process, because it helps the judge or the jury uncover the truth of the matter at hand. As one famous law professor wrote: "It is beyond doubt the greatest legal engine ever invented for the discovery of truth."[20]

Just one year earlier, in 1965, the Supreme Court had held that the Sixth Amendment right of confrontation and cross-examination applied to state adult criminal proceedings.[21] Dorsen's job, therefore, was to persuade the Court to recognize the same necessity for a "fair or reliable determination of truth" in juvenile matters.[22]

Once again, the extreme nature of what had happened in Globe—that Judge McGhee deprived Gerald of his liberty for *six years*, without hearing directly from Mrs. Cook, without knowing precisely what Gerald was alleged to have said, and without giving Gerald any opportunity to challenge or question her—flew in the face of any common definition of due process. Dorsen forcefully argued this point, drawing on the growing number of state courts that had recognized the right of confrontation and cross-examination in juvenile and other types of noncriminal proceedings.

In addition, Dorsen posed a direct challenge to the finding of the Arizona Supreme Court that the right of confrontation becomes important only when a child denies the charges of delinquency. Judge McGhee testified at the habeas corpus hearing that he did not believe that it was necessary to call Mrs. Cook to testify, since Gerald and

Ronald had admitted making the statements. This ruling turned topsy-turvy the idea of a trial, in which the court must hear and weigh all of the evidence and then make a decision, and relieved the probation officer or prosecutor of the burden of having to prove the charges at all.

Privilege Against Self-Incrimination. The Fifth Amendment of the United States Constitution states: "No person shall be compelled in a criminal case to be a witness against himself." This right is commonly known as the "privilege against self-incrimination." It means that a person cannot be forced to testify in court or give information to the police that can later be used against him.

The Arizona Juvenile Code that was in place in 1966 allowed *any* child under the age of eighteen years to be prosecuted as an adult. Although all children charged with a crime initially went before the juvenile court, the juvenile judge could decide, after an adjudication hearing—an informal trial on the charges—to refuse to consider the child as a delinquent but, instead, refer the child to the adult criminal court.[23] There, a new trial might be held, and whatever the young person said to the probation officer or the juvenile court judge could be used against him or her in that proceeding. As a result, when Gerald was forced to testify on June 9, he ran a very real risk of criminal prosecution, yet neither Judge McGhee nor Officer

Flagg told him that he had a right not to answer questions or of the potential consequences of doing so.

Dorsen relied heavily on this possibility of criminal prosecution in arguing that the privilege against self-incrimination should apply to juvenile delinquency proceedings. He urged the Court to make clear that "if a state allows the risk of self-incrimination to arise in its juvenile proceedings, it must afford the privilege [against self- incrimination] to the juvenile."[24] In addition, he roundly rejected the Arizona Supreme Court's finding that extending the privilege to delinquency cases would undermine the treatment goals of the juvenile court. Because there was a clear distinction between the two stages of a delinquency case, the privilege could be protected during the adjudication hearing. Once the young person was found guilty of the offense, however, the court could focus on questions of treatment and rehabilitation.

Right to Transcript and Appellate Review. Finally, Dorsen turned to the two related questions of whether children found guilty of delinquency had a right to have a transcript or tape recording made of the juvenile court hearings and whether they had a right to appeal the juvenile court's decision. The importance of these two questions is illustrated well by the transcript of Gerald Gault's habeas corpus hearing in August 1964, a short two months after Judge McGhee decided his fate. Gerald's parents, Officer Flagg, and Judge McGhee all testified at the habeas corpus hearing, but they remembered different things about what had been said during the hearings of June 9 and 13. In addition, even though Judge McGhee testified that he based his decision largely on Gerald's own statements, he could not remember what those statements were or exactly what Gerald had admitted doing. Because no transcript was kept, no record existed of these critical factors, making it impossible for a higher court to determine whether Judge McGhee decided the case correctly.

Unlike the other protections that Dorsen was seeking for Gerald Gault and other young people, however, neither the right to a transcript nor the right to appeal has ever been recognized by the Supreme Court to be constitutionally mandated in state criminal cases. Thus, Dorsen was forced to rely on much broader arguments about the meaning of due process to make these claims. With regard to appellate review, he asserted that the broad powers of juvenile court judges, and the relaxed nature of juvenile court hearings, made appellate review "extremely important." The judicial system, in other words, must protect fairness by ensuring that higher courts check and control lower ones.[25]

Similarly, without a transcript, it was impossible to challenge the actions of a juvenile court judge, because memory is often faulty and what actually happened or was said in the juvenile court is easily lost, leaving the actions of the court immune from challenge. The only way to ensure a reliable retelling of what occurred in the juvenile court was to require a transcript of those hearings.

After Dorsen finished drafting the brief, Daniel Rezneck carefully revised it, and then Dorsen revised it some more. When they were finished, Dorsen was "very satisfied" with the effort and was "reasonably confident that this was a winning case."[26] Lawyers for the state of Arizona, of course, felt otherwise.

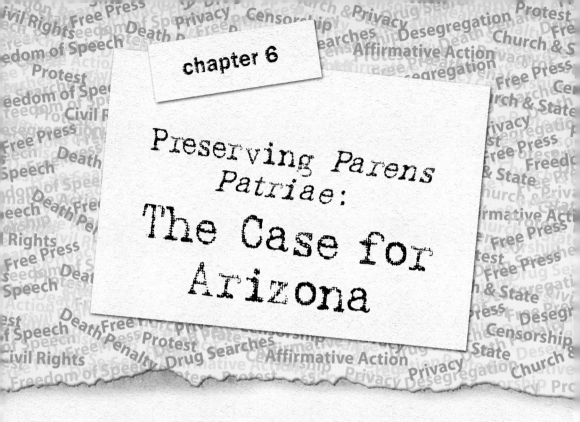

chapter 6

Preserving Parens Patriae: The Case for Arizona

How did the state of Arizona respond to Dorsen and Rezneck's arguments? As might be expected, the state's goal was to persuade the Supreme Court to uphold the constitutionality of its Juvenile Code and the informal processes of its juvenile courts. This argument was rooted, of course, in the idealistic vision of Jane Addams's Children's Court, and a belief in the *parens patriae* philosophy.

Lawyers who represent governmental agencies or institutions often are called "attorneys general." Representing Arizona before the Supreme Court was an assistant attorney general named Frank Parks. Only thirty years old in 1966, Parks had become an attorney just one year earlier and was one of the youngest and least experienced lawyers in his office.[1] Because the Supreme Court hears only a small number of cases each year, most American lawyers go through their entire careers without ever having the opportunity to argue a case there. That Parks took on the *Gault* case at such a young age, with no prior Supreme Court experience, was striking. The assignment would have intimidated much more seasoned lawyers.

The State's Argument

Like the brief written by Norman Dorsen and Daniel Rezneck, the state of Arizona's brief centered around one overarching question: Did Judge McGhee (and, by extension, the Arizona Juvenile Code) give Gerald Gault due process of law? Not surprisingly, and in contrast to Gerald's attorneys, Frank Parks answered this question with a resounding "Yes."

Parks began by embracing the tradition and history of a juvenile court based on the *parens patriae* philosophy. The unique character of the juvenile court would be destroyed, he argued, "if injected with the rights of due process as construed in the criminal system."[2] He then traced a long history of similar challenges to the juvenile codes of other states, in which objections similar to those raised by the Gaults and the ACLU had been rejected. Because a finding of juvenile delinquency is not a criminal conviction, and because the juvenile court had the authority not to punish but to rehabilitate, the constitutional protections normally enjoyed by adult defendants—such as the right to counsel, the right to trial by jury, and the privilege against self-incrimination—were not necessary and, in fact, might be harmful in juvenile cases. Rather than the specific protections of the Bill of Rights, due process for juveniles required only "fundamental fairness."

Parks noted that in other states, juvenile codes similar to that of Arizona had been upheld. Citing the Pennsylvania Supreme Court in the case of *In re Holmes*, he wrote:

> Such claims [of unconstitutionality], however, entirely overlook . . . the basic concept of a juvenile court. Proceedings in such a court are not in the nature of a criminal trial but constitute merely a civil inquiry or action looking to the treatment, reformation and the rehabilitation of the minor child. Their purpose is not penal but protective,—aimed to check juvenile delinquency and to throw around a child, just starting, perhaps, on an evil course and deprived of proper parental care, the strong arm of the state acting as *parens patriae*.[3]

Because Judge McGhee had followed the Arizona Code in adjudicating and sentencing Gerald Gault, Parks argued, the Gaults had in fact received due process of law.

Other, more specific arguments followed. Parks took on each of the rights asserted by the ACLU and argued either that (1) the Gaults had received sufficient protection in the Gila County Family Court, or (2) the Constitution did not extend the right in question to children or their parents in juvenile delinquency proceedings. He also maintained that extending these additional protections to children would undermine the workings of the juvenile justice system.

On the question of notice of the charges and the hearing, Parks argued that Probation Officer Flagg's statements to Mrs. Gault at the detention home, together with his handwritten note on June 12, were sufficient. He acknowledged that if Gerald had denied making the telephone call to Mrs. Cook, he and his parents might have needed more time to prepare for the hearing. Since Gerald admitted making the call to the judge, however, the Gaults received adequate warning. (Of course, if Gerald had been represented by a lawyer or had been warned of his privilege against self-incrimination—two of the other protections that Dorsen sought—this reasoning would not have held true.)

With regard to the right to counsel, Parks urged the Court again to maintain the historical nature of the juvenile court. If children were entitled to have a defense lawyer, the state would then have to be represented by a prosecuting attorney, and the proceedings would become argumentative and adversarial rather than informal and rehabilitative. Parks flatly rejected Dorsen's argument that a defense attorney was critically necessary to conduct investigations, interview witnesses, give legal advice, and conduct the defense, asserting instead that the probation officer could perform these tasks. Finally, he argued once again that because juvenile proceedings were not technically criminal cases, children enjoyed only a right to "fairness" rather than the Sixth Amendment's specific guarantee of a defense lawyer, and reminded the Court that if a juvenile judge felt it necessary, he or she could permit a young person to be represented by counsel in a particular case.

Parks made a different argument altogether with regard to the right of confrontation and cross-examination. He asserted that because Gerald had admitted making the telephone call to Mrs. Cook, there would have been nothing about which to cross-examine her, and, therefore, that he was not prejudiced by her absence. The rights of confrontation and cross-examination only came into play, he argued, when the young person denied the charges.

The privilege against self-incrimination not only protects criminal defendants from being forced to testify but also requires that courts and police officers tell them of that right. Contrary to Dorsen's argument that the privilege should apply in juvenile delinquency proceedings, Parks asserted that the treatment goals of the juvenile court would be defeated if children were discouraged from admitting their guilt:

> The first purpose of a hearing is to learn the truth. Which is the greater justice to the child: to teach him honesty and encourage him to reveal the truth or to pave the way for him to lie and conceal the truth? Doctors diagnose and treat the child whose body is sick. The child is never encouraged to deceive the doctor or to evade his questions. Must there be a different ethic when a child's behavior is sick?[4]

The state of Arizona argued for the constitutionality of its juvenile justice system, which had sent Gerald Gault to the Fort Grant Industrial School, shown above.

Because the job of juvenile court judges is in part to treat "sick" behavior, Parks wrote, they should not be required to warn children of the potential consequences of confessing.

Parks's arguments regarding the privilege against self-incrimination are particularly interesting in light of *Miranda* v. *Arizona*, the critically important case decided by the U.S. Supreme Court only one year earlier.[5] *Miranda* required police officers to warn suspects of their right to remain silent and of their right to have a lawyer present at any interrogation. The Arizona Attorney General's office, which had argued against the creation of these rules, was still smarting from its defeat in *Miranda*. In fact, its position in *Gault* may be seen in part as an attempt to limit the breadth of the *Miranda* ruling.

Finally, Parks turned to the question of the right to a transcript of juvenile court proceedings and the right to appeal from a decision of the juvenile court. Not surprisingly, he maintained that children who have been found to be delinquent do not have the right to appeal and, consequently, that there was neither a right to nor a need for a transcript of delinquency proceedings.

Parks relied on earlier decisions of both the Arizona and United States Supreme Courts in arguing that appeals are not available as a matter of right but of "grace." By this, he meant that it was up to state legislatures to decide whether the right to appeal should be included in their juvenile codes, and that failure to extend that right to children did not violate the Constitution. In addition, because a process, called *certiorari*, did exist in Arizona for a limited number of juvenile cases to be reviewed by higher courts (although it was left to those courts to decide whether or not to accept the case), no further appellate rights were necessary. And because the only purpose of a transcript is to pre-serve the proceedings for future appeals (and because juvenile proceedings were deemed to be confidential), due process was not violated by the failure to transcribe juvenile delinquency hearings.

With their briefs completed, Dorsen and Parks turned their attention to the Supreme Court oral argument of the case, scheduled for December 6, 1966. The fate of America's juvenile courts, and the children they served, hung in the balance.

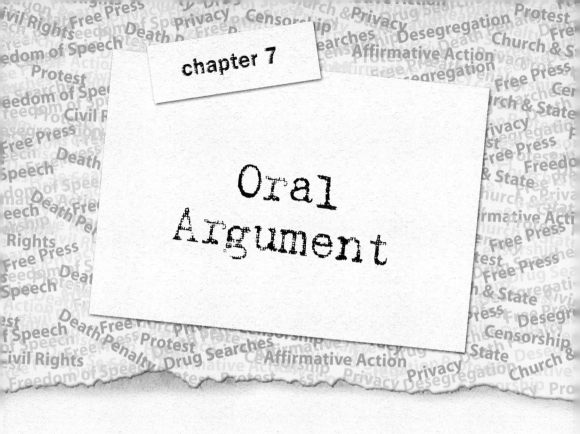

chapter 7

Oral Argument

On December 6, 1966, Norman Dorsen and Frank Parks found themselves seated at the burnished wood attorneys' tables in the stately chamber of the United States Supreme Court in Washington, D.C. Both were in their thirties, and it was the first Supreme Court appearance for both men. That either lawyer was there at all was, in many ways, a stroke of luck. Because the Court hears such a small number of cases each year, for most lawyers, having the chance to argue before the Court is often a matter of being in the right place at the right time.

Even though his case was about to be heard by the highest court in the land, Gerald Gault was back in Globe, living with his parents. After six months at Fort Grant, he was sent home in December 1964 under Arizona's "home placement program" and never had any other trouble with the law. He was still under the supervision of the Arizona authorities, however, and could have been sent back to Fort Grant if he misbehaved.

Appearances in the Supreme Court are called oral arguments. Strict rules govern how oral argument is conducted. In 1966, each side was given one full hour to plead its case to the Court. (Today, the time has been cut to thirty minutes.) The nine justices sit at a high bench at the front of the room, and they usually pepper the lawyers with questions. Often, it is possible to predict how a justice will vote on a case by the tone of his or her questions.

The Supreme Court of Earl Warren

In December 1966, the Chief Justice of the Supreme Court was Earl Warren, and the Court of that time is widely referred to as the "Warren Court." In addition to the usual work of a justice of the Supreme Court—hearing cases, reading briefs and other documents, and writing opinions—the Chief Justice is responsible for making sure that the Court runs smoothly and that enough agreement is reached on important issues to ensure that the law of the land is clear. The Chief Justice also, in many ways, sets the tone for the Court.

In addition to Chief Justice Warren, eight other justices sat on the Court: John Marshall Harlan, Hugo Black, William O. Douglas, William Brennan, Tom Clark, Potter Stewart, Byron White, and Abe Fortas.

After oral argument is held on a case, the Court holds a conference. Secrecy is the rule of the conference; only the nine justices are permitted to be in the room. During the conference, the justices discuss their views of the case and vote on its outcome. Supreme Court cases are decided by a majority vote; if five justices vote to overturn a lower court's ruling, then the ruling is reversed. If the majority decides that the lower court's decision was correct, it is affirmed. If the vote is a tie (because a justice is absent or has excused himself or herself from the deliberations), the lower court ruling is upheld.

After the conference, one justice writes the opinion for the majority. If the decision was not unanimous, a justice who disagrees with the outcome writes a dissenting opinion. Frequently, justices agree with the outcome but disagree with the reasoning of the majority, and will write concurring opinions setting forth their own views. Similarly, a justice might be in the minority but still write a separate dissenting opinion. All of these opinions, but particularly that of the majority, are crucially important, because they explain the

Court's reasoning and state the principles and ideas that make up American constitutional law.

Often, Supreme Court justices will become interested in a particular legal issue. Justice Abe Fortas, who had been on the Court for less than two years at the time *Gault* was argued, had already established himself as the Court's "expert" on juvenile justice and the right to counsel. His interest in the right to counsel had begun five years earlier, when he was a prominent lawyer in Washington, D.C., and was asked by the Court to represent James Earl Gideon in his quest to establish the right to counsel for poor criminal defendants.[1] Fortas successfully argued that case, *Gideon* v. *Wainwright*. After he was appointed to the Court in 1965, he wrote the majority opinion in *Kent*. It thus was clear that Fortas might well take a leading role in both the oral argument and the Court's ultimate decision in *In re Gault*.

Presenting the Argument for Gault

Because he represented the appellant, or the person bringing the appeal, Norman Dorsen stood up to argue first. He began by telling Gerald Gault's story, emphasizing the facts that best demonstrated the gross unfairness of what had happened in Arizona. He underscored the conflicting memories of Mrs. Gault, Officer Flagg, and Judge McGhee in order to highlight the critical need for a transcript,

Chief Justice Earl Warren led the Supreme Court from 1953 to 1969. During that time, the Court expanded the protections of the Bill of Rights.

reminding the Court that Judge McGhee had testified that although the case was decided "solely" on the basis of Gerald's confession, no one could remember exactly what Gerald had said. He pointed out that, although Gerald was adjudicated and sent to the training school on the basis of his statements alone, he was never warned of his right not to say anything or of the possible negative consequences of speaking. Dorsen also argued that Gerald was harmed by not being informed of the exact charge against him, because he could not properly defend himself. At this, Justice Fortas asked Dorsen, "Are you clear about the charge?" Dorsen replied, "Your honor, even the judge wasn't clear about the charge!"[2]

The main focus of Dorsen's argument was the right to counsel. He dismissed the claim made by the state of Arizona that probation officers adequately protected the rights of children, noting that Officer Flagg signed the petition of delinquency against Gerald and was the only witness for the prosecution at the adjudication hearing. Because Flagg was acting as Gerald's adversary throughout most of the case, he could not possibly protect Gerald's interests effectively. Dorsen argued that the absence of defense lawyers does not guarantee harmonious and informal juvenile courts but, instead, created a one-sided, biased system "rife with conflicts."[3] He further asserted that the right to counsel was, in many ways, more important for children than adults, because children are less able to understand the court process or conduct any sort of a legal defense.

When asked whether other states already guaranteed the rights that should have been granted to Gerald in Arizona, Dorsen was quick to point out that thirty-seven, or 74 percent, of the states had extended the right to counsel to juveniles. He also noted that New York's Family Court Act specifically provided for counsel, a written transcript, and the right to appeal. He also distinguished between the adjudication and disposition, or sentencing, stages of delinquency cases, noting that certain protections were necessary for adjudication but not for disposition.

The Court's questions to Dorsen sent a strong signal that most, if not all, of the justices agreed with his position. Although most of the questions came from Justice Fortas, others also weighed in. Chief Justice Warren asked, "Did the boy have a record?" and appeared quite satisfied to learn that the answer was no.[4] The Court had a number of questions about Fort Grant: What were the conditions there? Was it only for delinquent children, or for neglected children, too? Was it a secure, or locked, facility? Were Gerald's parents allowed to take him home? And, in what may have been the question with the greatest impact on the Court, Justice Fortas asked what punishment an adult could have received for the same offense. Dorsen answered, "Two months." Justice Fortas inquired, "And this boy received?" Dorsen replied, "Six years." A brief silence followed.[5]

The State Responds

The presentation by Frank Parks focused on maintaining the *parens patriae* philosophy of the juvenile court. He asserted that children are different from adults and that their freedom is limited. They are not permitted to drive or to enter into contracts, and until the end of adolescence they are controlled by their parents. When a parent is not doing his or her job, it was the state's job to do it in the parent's place, and that the juvenile court was "the State's last opportunity to make a child a good citizen."[6] Because due process rights for young people would interfere with the state's goal of individualized treatment, he argued, the Court should not recognize them.

From the moment Parks began his argument, it was clear that most of the Court was skeptical about Arizona's position. The justices questioned him vigorously throughout the hour on a number of points. When Parks argued that Officer Flagg's oral statements to Mrs. Gault on June 9, when she tracked Gerald down at the detention home, were legally sufficient notice of the charges, Justice Fortas asked, "By what authority did the State detain the boy?" Parks replied, "Both parents were working and the boy was home alone." Chief Justice Warren then asked, "Was any written notice left at home?" When Parks tried to justify the lack of written notice by explaining that Officer Flagg was gone from the detention home all day and could not contact Mrs. Gault, Chief Justice Warren shot back, "But the police officers [who arrested Gerald] left no notice. His mother had to get the information from the neighbors."[7]

Regarding the contents of any notice that the Gaults might have received, Justice Fortas pointed out that although Judge McGhee testified at the habeas hearing that he based his decision in part on the earlier incident in which Gerald was accused of stealing a baseball glove, neither Gerald nor his parents were told during the June 1964 hearings that the judge was considering that incident. Parks replied that because the same judge and probation officer had been involved, written notice was not required. Justice Fortas pointed out that the judge himself could not remember the facts of that incident and that "an unwritten, unknown, and perhaps denied prior incident was the basis of locking a boy up for six years when an adult would have received two months."[8]

As for the right to counsel, Parks argued that judges should be able to decide whether or not to appoint a lawyer for a child who could not afford one, but that if a family that could afford to do so wished to hire a lawyer, it should be allowed to do so. In light of the Court's decision in *Gideon* v. *Wainwright* four years earlier, this position was sure to provoke a reaction, and it did. Chief Justice Warren quickly pointed out that such a system would "push on the distinction between rich and poor" that *Gideon* was meant to eliminate. Parks replied, "This is a concept of fair play."[9] It was now up to the justices to decide what "fair play" really meant in juvenile court.

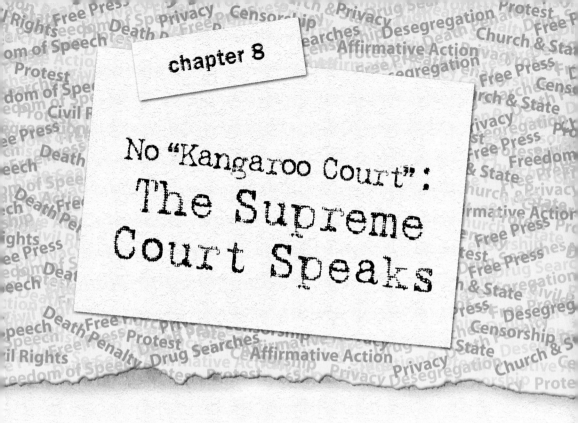

chapter 8

No "Kangaroo Court": The Supreme Court Speaks

On May 15, 1967, the United States Supreme Court announced its decision in the *Gault* case. After nearly three years, Marjorie and Paul Gault's firm belief that their son had been treated unfairly was rewarded. The Court held that the Arizona Juvenile Code violated the United States Constitution, and that Gerald Gault had been denied due process by the Arizona courts.

Although a clear majority of eight justices voted to extend the Fourteenth Amendment's guarantee of due process to children in delinquency matters, the Court was split in its reasoning. As might have been expected, Justice Abe Fortas wrote the majority opinion, in which Chief Justice Warren and Justices Brennan, Clark, and Douglas joined. Justices Black and White wrote concurring opinions, Justice Harlan partly concurred and partly dissented, and Justice Stewart wrote a dissent.

Justice Fortas began, as Dorsen had, by summarizing the facts of the case—and, so, reaffirming that even complicated legal questions and theories arise out of real people dealing with real problems. He then turned to the history of the juvenile court. Even if the ideal of the *parens patriae* approach made sense in certain legal situations, he wrote, it created serious dangers in delinquency cases:

> The absence of . . . standards has not necessarily meant that children receive careful, compassionate, individualized treatment. The absence of procedural rules . . . has not always produced fair, efficient, and effective procedures. . . . Failure to observe the fundamental requirements of due process has resulted in instances, which might have been avoided, of unfairness to individuals and inadequate or inaccurate findings of fact. . . . [1]

Drawing on the many studies and reports that had been made about the juvenile court system, Justice Fortas asserted that it simply was no longer working. Young people who went through the system were often rearrested, and they often suffered the same or harsher consequences as adults. Although juvenile proceedings were supposed to be confidential, the names of and information about children who had been arrested were regularly provided to the FBI and other law enforcement agencies, as well as the military and private employers. Counseling and other help that was supposed to be provided to delinquent children either was not available or was ineffective. In short, the differences between juvenile and criminal proceedings were shrinking rapidly and no longer could be used to justify the denial of basic protections and fairness.

Fortas went on to state that because children who, like Gerald, are sent to training schools in fact lose their liberty, and because they are involuntarily taken from their families, the Constitution must require meaningful due process. Had Gerald Gault been over eighteen at the time he made the infamous telephone call, he would have been fined no more than fifty dollars or sent to jail for no more than two months, but he would have been entitled to the full range of due process rights contained in the Constitution. Because he was merely fifteen, however, he would receive none of those protections but could be incarcerated for up to six years. In some of the most immortal words ever written by a Supreme Court justice, "Under our Constitution, the condition of being a boy does not justify a kangaroo court."[2]

After holding squarely that children who were charged with delinquency were "people" and so were entitled to due process under the Fourteenth Amendment, Justice Fortas discussed each of the rights asserted by Dorsen in turn. Notice must be given *in writing*, stating the specific charges and factual accusations that will be considered at a hearing and given to the *child and his parents or guardian* enough in advance of the hearing to permit them to prepare adequately.

The Court was steadfast in affirming the importance of the right to counsel. Justice Fortas roundly dismissed the notion that probation officers could represent the interests of children in court, noting that in Arizona, probation officers are the arresting officers, the petitioners, witnesses against the child, and, in the case of Officer Flagg, the supervisor of the detention home. It is impossible for someone who takes so many actions against the child to also act as counsel for that child. In addition, Justice Fortas pointed out that state legislators, court decisions, and legal experts from across the country had recognized the critical importance of counsel for children. Thus, the Court held that in cases where a child might be sent to an institution, *the child and his or her parent* must be notified of the child's right to be represented by an attorney, and of the right to have an attorney paid for by the state if the family could not afford to hire one.

Justice Fortas next considered the privilege

against self-incrimination and the right of confrontation and cross-examination together. Regarding self-incrimination, the Court focused on concerns that had not even been raised by Dorsen. The methods that police use to question suspects can be very intimidating, especially to children, and children who feel threatened are more likely to say things that are not true in order to stop the questioning. The Court had previously recognized this problem and had long questioned whether confessions by young people were trustworthy.[3] In addition, even though delinquency proceedings were not technically the same as criminal prosecutions, the potential consequences of a delinquency adjudication were severe enough to require similar protections. Based on these and other considerations, the Court found the Fifth Amendment to apply to juvenile delinquency matters. Consequently, children must be warned not only of the privilege but also of their right to speak with any attorney before they waive the privilege (that is, choose to speak anyway).

Given that Gerald's "confession" was unreliable, Justice Fortas wrote that the Family Court needed additional evidence before it could find Gerald to be delinquent. In order for the Family Court to consider Mrs. Cook's statements consistently with due process, she needed to be present in court, swear to tell the truth, and be cross-examined by

Gerald or his lawyer. These would have been the requirements of a criminal trial, and "no reason is suggested or appears for a different rule in respect of sworn testimony in juvenile courts than in adult tribunals."[4]

Finally, Justice Fortas turned to the question of transcripts and appellate review. Here, however, the Court drew the line. Even though the facts of *Gault* made clear the importance of a written record of court proceedings, and although habeas corpus proceedings were much more complicated than appeals, the Court had not yet found that the Constitution required the right of appeal in state criminal cases. Thus, and because the case was being reversed for other reasons, the Court refused to make a ruling on these two claims.

Concurring Opinions and Dissents

The other opinions written in the *Gault* case—two concurring, one dissenting, and one partly concurring and partly dissenting—reveal something of the discussion that the justices must have had during the case conference and about how they struggled with the many issues raised by the case. Justice Hugo Black was worried that the case would destroy the unique nature of the juvenile court but agreed that because children could in fact be incarcerated, the Constitution applied equally to them and adults. Justice Byron White also agreed with the extension of due process rights to children generally, but disagreed that Gerald Gault's privilege against self-incrimination had been violated. This was because there was no transcript of the delinquency proceeding showing what Gerald had said, and because the delinquency hearing occurred in 1964, before *Miranda* v. *Arizona* established that courts and police must warn people of the privilege and the potential consequences of speaking.

Justice Abe Fortas wrote the majority opinion in the Gault *case, stating: "The condition of being a boy does not justify a kangaroo court."*

Justice John Harlan partly concurred and partly dissented in the outcome. He agreed that some due process rights applied to juvenile delinquency cases, but he would not go as far as the majority. He would have limited the protections to those three that, he said, were necessary to ensure "fundamental fairness": notice of the charges, the right to counsel, and (interestingly) right to a written transcript and appeal. The privilege against self-incrimination and rights to confrontation and cross-examination would, he felt, significantly change juvenile proceedings and destroy the unique nature of the juvenile court.

Finally, Justice Potter Stewart strongly dissented: "I believe that the Court's decision is wholly unsound as a matter of constitutional law, and sadly unwise as a matter of judicial policy." He maintained that juvenile proceedings were neither criminal nor civil nor even adversarial proceedings, because their purpose was, in his words, "correction of a condition" rather than punishing a criminal act. Even though the juvenile court had failed to live up to its promise and to the hopes and dreams of the early reformers, he said, he was "certain that the answer does not lie in the Court's opinion in this case, which serves to convert a juvenile proceeding into a criminal prosecution."[5]

Stewart used a nineteenth-century case involving a twelve-year-old boy named James Guild to drive home his point. James was accused of murder, and, because there was no juvenile court at the time, he was tried in a criminal court. "A jury found him guilty of murder, and he was sentenced to death by hanging. The sentence was executed. It was all very constitutional."[6] Although he recognized that certain basic due process protections must apply ("I suppose that all would agree that a brutally coerced confession could not constitutionally be considered in a juvenile court"), he objected to requiring strict and formal procedures in juvenile courts.

Despite these observations, Justice Stewart

dissented for a different reason. Because he agreed with the Arizona Supreme Court that Gerald's parents knew of their right to counsel, had adequate notice, and understood that they could call Mrs. Cook to testify and cross-examine her, he felt that they were not harmed in any way, and would have simply dismissed the appeal.

The Court's decision in *Gault* established a new constitutional framework for the juvenile court. The next forty years would bring a rash of other developments in both the courts and in state legislatures, which reflected both Justice Fortas's and Justice Stewart's assumptions about the post-*Gault* juvenile justice system. The question remains, even today: Who was right?

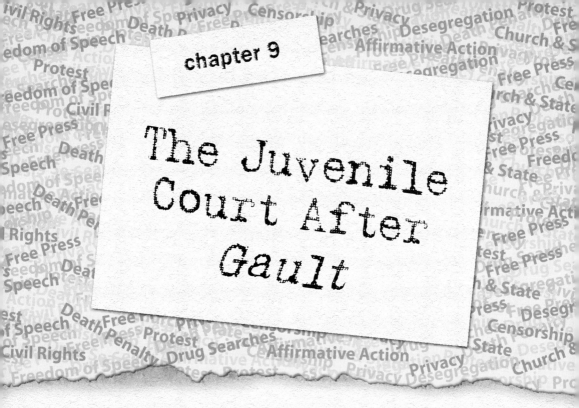

chapter 9

The Juvenile Court After Gault

Have American juvenile courts lived up to the promise of *In re Gault*? Do children who are caught up in the juvenile justice system today enjoy the perfect balance of procedural fairness and individualized treatment envisioned by Justice Fortas, or have we taken the "long step backwards into the nineteenth century" feared by Justice Stewart? If Gerald Gault were to be brought before a juvenile court today, how would he be treated?

Nearly forty years after the Supreme Court issued its decision, the answers to these questions are complex and somewhat sobering. The experiences of children caught up in the juvenile justice system vary widely, depending on where they live, the color of their skin, and a host of other factors. After a decade of expanding the definition of due process for children, the Supreme Court began to pull back with a series of decisions that refused to extend other constitutional rights to juveniles. Increasingly negative public opinions about youth crime in the 1990s led to the passage of new laws in almost every state imposing harsher punishments, stripping away privacy protections, and requiring that more young people be tried in the adult criminal system. In fact, at the time of the one-hundredth anniversary of the juvenile court in 1999, a number of American scholars and politicians were demanding that it be abolished.

Right to Counsel

The main challenge posed by the Supreme Court's decision lay in its mandate that young people charged with delinquency have meaningful legal representation. In order for juvenile courts to comply with this requirement, they had to do at least four things: (1) notify children that they have a right to be represented by an attorney, and that a lawyer would be appointed by the court if they and their parents could not afford to hire one; (2) make juvenile defense attorneys readily available to young people, through a local public defender office or other means; (3) ensure that children facing delinquency charges do not waive their right to counsel without fully understanding the dangers of that decision; and (4) ensure that juvenile defenders provide competent and effective legal representation to their clients.

Obviously, the first challenge for juvenile courts across the country was to develop systems for providing lawyers to children whose parents could not afford one—the overwhelming majority of young people who come before the courts. In *Gideon* v. *Wainwright*, the Supreme Court gave states the right to shape their own system of defense representation for poor adults. Most states (as well as the federal government) have split this mammoth responsibility between public defenders, who work directly for the government, and private attorneys, who are paid by the government on a client-by-client basis. Because most states did not have juvenile public defender systems in 1967, particularly in rural areas, this requirement created significant difficulties for state and local governments as well as the courts. Unfortunately, even today, these challenges have not been met successfully.

Since 1967, when the Court issued its decision, enormous differences have existed in the availability and quality of legal representation for children in different parts of the country. A study conducted two years after *Gault*, in 1969, showed that while more than half of the children in one urban juvenile court were notified of their right to counsel, no children in another urban court were so advised. Similar problems were found in rural areas.[1] And because children who are not told that they have a right to a lawyer and offered an opportunity to meet with one are highly unlikely to seek out legal representation on their own, equally small numbers were ultimately represented in court. In fact, in 1988, Professor Barry Feld of the University of Minnesota found huge differences in rates of juvenile defense representation across the country: While more than 95 percent of the children charged with delinquency in New York State and Philadelphia were represented by a lawyer, only 37.5 percent of North Dakota's young people had counsel.[2]

Even among those children who did have a lawyer, there were vast differences noted in the amount of time, attention, skill, and passion that juvenile defenders devoted to their clients.[3] Largely because of the clear distinction *Gault* drew between the adjudication, or trial, stage of a delinquency case and the disposition, or treatment, stage, representing a child is, in many ways, more difficult for a lawyer than representing an adult criminal defendant. In addition to the usual tasks involved in criminal defense—crime scene investigation, legal preparation, cross-examination, closing arguments, and every other aspect of a trial—juvenile defenders must work to establish relationships with young clients and their families, gather documents related to the child's educational and treatment needs, identify assistance for the child outside of the local detention center or training school, and help the child plan for the future. These responsibilities are difficult enough to meet when a lawyer is representing only a few clients, but, because public defenders often have caseloads of more than one hundred children at a time, the job can become overwhelming.

As early as 1974, when it passed the Juvenile Justice and Delinquency Prevention Act, the United States Congress found that "understaffed, overcrowded juvenile courts, probation services, and correctional facilities are not able to provide individualized justice or effective help."[4] Later versions of this law specifically noted the shortcomings of juvenile defender offices.[5]

By the early 1990s, concern over the question of juvenile defense grew so great that a national study of access to counsel and quality of representation for juveniles was conducted.[6] As its authors ultimately concluded, "Obviously, the promise of *In re Gault* . . . has yet to be fulfilled."[7] Juvenile public defenders had huge caseloads, often exceeding five hundred clients per year. These high caseloads, which were the result of persistently inadequate funding for defense services, were the "single most important barrier to effective representation," affecting every aspect of the attorney's relationship with and work on behalf of clients. There is no time to meet with clients, investigate the family or the legal defense, or obtain necessary information. As a result, children are detained unnecessarily and "receive the clear impression that their attorneys do not care about them and are not going to make any effort on their behalf." One child stated that his detention hearing "went like a conveyor belt."[8]

These problems are even worse in those courts that do not even appoint a juvenile defender until *after* the first detention hearing, when what is perhaps the most important decision of the case is made. Like Gerald Gault, children today still are routinely sent to detention homes or centers without the benefit of a lawyer to argue for their release.

All too often, children waive their right to a lawyer altogether. This happens for a number of reasons. Sometimes, as stated above, juvenile court judges will not tell children that they have a right to a lawyer, and the children do not know. Because defense lawyers (if they are doing their job effectively) often slow down the proceedings, some judges discourage children from exercising their right to counsel. Parents also sometimes do not understand that public defender representation is free or low cost, and instruct their children to waive counsel for financial reasons. The study found that judges do not adequately advise children of the potential negative effects of waiver, and that many of the waivers of this fundamental constitutional right were not "knowing and voluntary." Of course, as Gerald Gault's experience made clear, children who are not represented by counsel are at a serious disadvantage and are likely to be denied other aspects of due process.

The study made a number of recommendations for improving access to counsel. These included caseload limits, earlier appointments of counsel, and better training and support for juvenile defenders. More than ten years later, however, the problems persist; recent studies of juvenile defense services in more than ten states have demonstrated that high caseloads, high rates of waiver of counsel, and inadequate resources continue to plague juvenile public defenders.[9] There is hope, however; a National Juvenile Defender Center has been created to provide training and support to juvenile defenders, and there seems to be a growing recognition of the critical importance and effectiveness of a skilled and vigorous juvenile defense system.

Supreme Court Cases After *Gault*

Although *In re Gault* addressed most of the elements of due process, there remained several protections given to adults but not yet to children. These included, among others, the requirement that the prosecution prove its case "beyond a reasonable doubt" and the right to a jury trial. The

Supreme Court was not asked to consider these questions in *Gault* but, in the years immediately following, both issues made their way to the Court, with mixed results.

The amount of evidence that is required to prove a legal claim differs according to the type of case involved. Plaintiffs in civil matters, which do not involve the threat of prison or negative effects of a criminal record, generally have to prove their cases by "preponderance of the evidence," meaning that it is more likely than not that the acts in question occurred. Since at least 1789, however, many American courts have required proof "beyond a reasonable doubt" in criminal cases because of the very serious penalties they involve. This requires significantly more proof than a preponderance of the evidence, but nevertheless is difficult to define precisely. The Massachusetts Supreme Court coined the most common definition in 1850:

> It is not a mere possible doubt; because everything relating to human affairs . . . is open to some possible or imaginary doubt. It is that state of the case, which, after the entire comparison and consideration of all the evidence, leaves the minds of jurors in that condition that they cannot say they feel an abiding conviction, to a moral certainty, of the truth of the charge.[10]

Despite the long acceptance of the "beyond a reasonable doubt" standard in criminal cases, the phrase is found in neither the Constitution nor the Bill of Rights. And, at the time *In re Gault* was decided, the United States Supreme Court had never held it to be the law of the land.

In the late 1960s, most states—even those like New York, which had already incorporated due process protections into its juvenile code—permitted delinquency cases (which are technically considered to be civil, not criminal) to be proven by a preponderance of the evidence. Other states (like Arizona, in fact) required proof by "clear and convincing evidence," a slightly higher standard.

The Supreme Court resolved this question in 1970 in *In re Winship*.[11] Twelve-year-old Samuel Winship had been arrested in New York City and charged with stealing a purse. Despite conflicting testimony at his trial in Family Court, and although Samuel's lawyer urged the court to employ the "beyond a reasonable doubt" standard, the judge found him to be a delinquent based on a preponderance of the evidence. When Samuel's case reached the Supreme Court, the Court held that fundamental fairness—the measure of due process used in *Kent* and *Gault*—requires that juvenile courts employ the "beyond a reasonable doubt" standard in determining whether a young person is guilty of delinquent activity. In fact, Justice William Brennan, who wrote the majority opinion, used the opportunity to declare explicitly that the Due Process Clause requires proof beyond a reasonable doubt for adult criminal defendants, as well.[12]

With *In re Winship*, the Court's four-year effort to reshape the juvenile justice system came to an end. The retirement of Chief Justice Earl Warren and resignation of Justice Abe Fortas led to the appointment of new justices and a marked change in the philosophy of the Court. In a series of cases throughout the 1970s and 1980s, the Court re-embraced the traditional view of the juvenile court and refused to incorporate additional Bill of Rights guarantees into the definition of "due process" in juvenile proceedings. In *McKeiver* v. *Pennsylvania*, for example, the Court refused to hold that the Sixth Amendment right to jury trials in criminal prosecutions extended to children charged with delinquency.[13] And, in *Schall* v. *Martin*, the Court circled back to the ideal of *parens patriae* in holding that unlike adults, children could be held in a detention center before trial if they pose a risk of committing other offenses during that time.[14]

Recently, the Supreme Court returned to the question of whether young people should be treated differently from adults. In *Roper* v. *Simmons*, the Court held that people who are under the age of eighteen at the time they commit their crimes cannot be sentenced to death.[15] The Court found that because most states prohibit sentencing young people to death, because international human rights laws forbid imposition of the death penalty on juveniles, and because scientific research has shown that adolescents have not yet developed full decision-making abilities, the juvenile death penalty constitutes "cruel and unusual punishment" and is forbidden by the United States Constitution.

New Laws

On the heels of the Supreme Court's return to a traditional view of the juvenile court, state legislatures across the country passed a wave of new laws that stripped away the historical differences between the adult criminal and juvenile justice systems. Owing in large part to a rise in juvenile crime rates between 1985 and 1992, "getting tough on youth crime" became a political slogan.

These changes took a number of forms. Every state in the nation enacted laws that increased the number of children tried in the adult system. Children can now be transferred to adult courts at younger ages and for less serious offenses than previously. Those who remain in the juvenile court are treated more harshly; in fact, a number of states have changed their juvenile codes to state that one of the purposes of the juvenile court is to "punish" rather than offer treatment to young people.

In addition to being punitive, these new laws operate unfairly. African-American young people, in particular, are affected unequally by the new laws. In comparison with white youth who engage in similar activity, they are more likely to be prosecuted in the adult system, more likely to be detained before trial, and more likely to receive a prison sentence.[16] Despite a federal law directing states to take actions to reduce the unfair treatment of minority youth, these problems persist.[17]

Traditionally, one of the main distinctions between the criminal and juvenile justice systems has been the confidentiality of juvenile proceedings. Because the main purpose of juvenile courts was to rehabilitate children who made youthful mistakes, they historically were closed to the public and the press. Reports and other documents remained confidential (secret), and, because they were not considered criminal convictions, findings of delinquency did not lead to a criminal record and could not be held against young people later in life; children were given a chance to learn from their mistakes and move on to become law-abiding adults.

The effort to criminalize delinquency, however, included laws that threw open juvenile courthouse doors and created permanent records of delinquency. In some states, delinquency cases were even allowed to be counted as "strikes" that could lead to life sentences without parole for crimes committed years later. Young people thus suffer the stigma of their past actions; they may be excluded from military or public service, find their names and photographs splashed across the local news, be turned down for jobs, and have their mistakes follow them into adulthood.

Even though the juvenile crime rate began falling in 1995 and continued to fall to record lows over the next decade, the laws passed in the 1990s remain on the books. They have fundamentally changed some of the basic principles of the juvenile justice system. Yet, the value of the juvenile court and the promise it holds remain clear.

In 1999, to celebrate the hundredth anniversary of Jane Addams's Children's Court, the Children's Court Centennial Project identified and interviewed a host of juvenile court "success stories." These included a former Olympian, politicians, a television reporter, lawyers, probation officers, and a host of other accomplished people. They talked about how the juvenile court system had given them a second chance, an opportunity to turn their lives around.[18] These opportunities would not have been available to them in a system that made their records public, or required them to be tried as adults, or mandated that they serve time in adult prisons.

What Happened to Gault?

Gerald Gault is also a success story. After returning home to Globe from Fort Grant, he went on to a career in the United States military. Eventually, he rose to the rank of sergeant. This path might not have been open to him had he been

Gerald Gault became a noncommissioned officer in the U.S. Army—a career that might not have been open to him if his case were to take place today. He is shown at an event honoring him and his attorney, Amelia Lewis.

prosecuted in today's juvenile court, where sentencing is harsher and children no longer are shielded by confidentiality.

In 1994, thirty years after he was taken from his family's house to the detention home, Gerald Gault spoke at a ceremony honoring Amelia Lewis, the attorney who bravely fought for his freedom in the courts of Arizona. He spoke of his confusion as he sat in Judge McGhee's courtroom and of how he simply did not understand what was happening to him until he realized that his six-year sentence was longer than he could count on the fingers of one hand. The promise of the case that bears his name is that children sitting in other juvenile courts across the country will no longer be confused, that they will have lawyers who are truly their champions, and that, whether guilty or innocent, they will be cloaked in the protections of the Constitution.

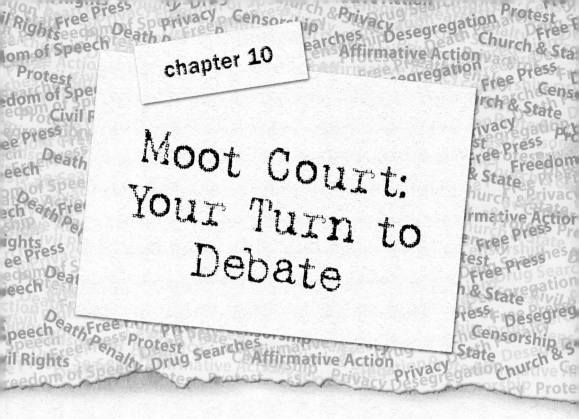

chapter 10

Moot Court: Your Turn to Debate

Now that you have learned about the arguments for and against extending Bill of Rights guarantees to juveniles, you are ready to hold a moot court proceeding of your own. Moot court is a pretend appellate argument. Students are given the facts of a real or hypothetical (fictional) case and the trial court's ruling. They research, write briefs, and argue legal issues before a make-believe panel of appeals court judges. The exercise hones research, writing, and debate skills.

Try a moot court activity with your class or club.[1] This activity deals with due process for children, but you can use the format to debate other legal issues, too.

Step 1: Assign Roles

Here are the roles you will need to fill:

◇ Judges. If the group is large enough, you can have nine justices like the Supreme Court has. Otherwise, have a panel of three appellate court judges. Choose one person to be the Chief Justice and direct the proceeding. The judges hear the attorneys' arguments, question them, and then write and deliver the final ruling. The court's majority opinion is the position agreed upon by a majority of the panel. Individual justices may choose to issue concurring or dissenting opinions of their own. If you want to, you can invite local lawyers to act as the judges.

◇ Two or more law clerks. They work with the justices to prepare five or more questions to ask the attorneys during oral arguments. Clerks also help the justices to research and write their opinions.

◇ A team of two or more attorneys for the appellant, who will argue that the lower court's ruling was wrong.

◇ A team of two or more attorneys for the appellee, who will argue that the lower court's ruling was correct.

◇ Each attorney team must choose a designated spokesperson to present the argument, but any of the attorneys may answer questions from the justices. Attorneys must address the major issues by presenting the most persuasive arguments for their side.

◇ Two or more reporters. They interview the attorneys before the case and write news stories about the facts of the case and the final ruling.

◇ The bailiff, who calls the Court to order. He or she will also time each side's oral argument.

Step 2: Prepare Your Case

Part 1: Review the Facts

Thirteen-year-old Violet Plant lived with her mother, four sisters, and two brothers in the poorest section of Elm City in the state of Sycamore. Her father died four years ago, and her mother has struggled to support the family ever since. Violet's mother works two jobs and, as a result, the children are forced to care for themselves.

Violet wanted to go to school regularly, but her mother often needed her to watch her younger siblings, and so Violet sometimes had trouble getting up on time. As a result, she was at risk of failing seventh grade. In addition, because Violet could not afford to buy new clothes or dress fashionably, other students often teased her.

One day last year, when money was so tight that she had not eaten anything since the day before, Violet was walking to school. She spotted two of the "cool" girls from her class, Ina Bullee and

Fraidie Katz, at the next corner. As soon as the girls saw Violet, they called out, "Where did you get those clothes, Vi—the dump?" At these words, something inside Violet snapped. She rushed toward the girls, jumped on Ina, and tried to pull her to the ground. Ina pulled free and began to hit Violet, and Violet, in turn, punched Ina. Fraidie started screaming, and, out of nowhere, a police officer appeared. He pulled Ina and Violet apart and asked Fraidie what happened. Fraidie told him that Violet had attacked Ina for no reason. The officer then arrested Violet, handcuffed her, and brought her in the police car to the station house.

At the station, the officer tried to contact Violet's mother but, because she was at work, she did not answer the telephone. Without telling Violet that she did not have to answer his questions or that she could speak with a lawyer before answering, the officer asked her whether she had hit Ina. Violet said, "Yes, but she always bullies me and she hit me first." The officer said, "Well, I guess you are going to have to see the judge." He then drove Violet to the Elm City Juvenile Court, where she was held in a locked room with four other young people for about three hours. During that time, Probation Officer Vera E. Friendly came and asked Violet questions about her family, school, the fight, and whether she had been in trouble before. Finally, a court officer came into the room, called out her name, and escorted her to a small courtroom.

Judge Justine Jurist sat at the front of the room behind a raised desk. Other people were in the room, too: a court reporter who was typing constantly, Probation Officer Friendly, and, at one of the two tables that faced the judge, a young man who was wearing a suit—the prosecuting attorney. Violet's mother sat at the other table, looking frightened and worried.

After Violet sat down, Judge Jurist said, "Violet, you are here because a complaint has been filed charging you with assaulting Ina Bullee. The complaint contains a statement made by Ina and a statement that you made to the police admitting that you hit her. I need to tell you that you can have a lawyer represent you in this case, but I think we could just as easily resolve it today without one." Violet's mother whispered to her, "Honey, I don't have any money to hire a lawyer." Violet's heart was pounding, and she felt like she was about to cry. She gulped and said, "All right."

The judge said, "We have a new program here in Elm City that helps young people like you stay out of trouble. If you plead guilty to the charge, I will place you on probation. You will have to see a probation officer once a week, go to a special school, and not get arrested again. We will also try to get some help for your mother and the rest of the family. At the end of two years, you will complete probation. If you don't follow the rules, however, you will have to come back to court and I could send you to the Sycamore State Training School." Violet agreed, admitted that she assaulted Ina, and, within fifteen minutes, was on her way home with her mother.

When Violet went to the new school, however, she found out that it was for students who were constantly in trouble. She felt like she was in jail. The probation officer yelled at her, threatening to send her to the training school. She also learned that because she pled guilty, she now had a record for juvenile delinquency that could prevent her from having certain jobs when she was older. To make matters worse, Ina teased her constantly now, taunting her about how she was the one who was in trouble.

Violet felt that she had not been treated fairly by Judge Jurist and the juvenile court. She wanted to erase what had been done, but the probation officer told her that this was not possible. Finally, her mother went to the local legal aid office, where a lawyer agreed to help her appeal the delinquency case. The basis for the appeal was that Violet was denied due process because she did not have a lawyer representing her in the juvenile court and because she did not understand what was happening when the judge asked her to waive her right to counsel. An assistant attorney general for the state of Sycamore argued that Violet in fact knowingly waived her right to a lawyer. The state also asserted that because Violet had not been sent to the training school but, instead, was receiving help from the juvenile court, her liberty was not at stake and the requirements of *In re Gault* did not apply to her.

The state of Sycamore appellate courts all upheld the juvenile court. The United States Supreme Court, well aware of the juvenile court system's ongoing failure to live up to the promise of *Gault*, has agreed to hear Violet's case in the upcoming term. One team of attorneys from your group will represent Violet, and the other lawyer team will represent the state of Sycamore.

Part 2: Gather Information

In 1967, the Supreme Court held in *In re Gault* that children charged with juvenile delinquency have a right to certain due process protections. These included the right to counsel, notice of the charges and hearings, confrontation and cross-examination, and the privilege against self-incrimination. Although eight justices agreed that children were entitled to due process, however, they were somewhat divided over exactly what "due process" meant in the context of juvenile court. As a result, three justices wrote separate concurring opinions. In addition, the ninth justice, Potter

Stewart, vehemently disagreed with the outcome of the case. He wrote a dissent favoring the traditional, *parens patriae* approach to juvenile justice.

Gault became legal precedent when the Court issued its opinion. For the last four decades, it has, at least in theory, controlled what can and cannot happen in juvenile courts in the United States. Many of the problems that plagued juvenile courts in 1967, however, still persist today, and serious doubts exist about whether the promise of *Gault* has been fulfilled.

Sometimes, the Supreme Court will revisit issues or questions that it decided previously. This happens because new laws are passed that may not comply with the Court's prior decisions, or because new justices with different legal philosophies are appointed to the Court, or because public opinions and attitudes about the topic have shifted in a dramatic and fundamental way. The Court may clarify its previous rulings or, occasionally, even overrule an earlier decision. The state of Sycamore, which is the appellee in your moot court exercise, is asking the Court to overrule or limit the holding of *Gault*. Violet, the appellant, is asking the Court to enforce it.

Everyone in your moot court activity should look at the *Gault* case. It is available on the Internet, or you may be able to find it in your public library. The Supreme Court's opinions can be found at 387 U.S. 1, which is volume 387 of *United*

States Reports, page 1. If your library has the *Supreme Court Reporter*, the case can be found in volume 87, page 1428. In addition, you might wish to look at *McKeiver* v. *Pennsylvania*, in which the Supreme Court denied children the right to trial by jury. The opinion discusses the other side of the *Gault* argument. The case is found in volume 403 of *United States Reports*, page 528.

You may also want to do additional research on the juvenile justice system. A good resource is the Web site of the National Juvenile Defender Center. This site provides links to other juvenile justice sites as well.

Part 3: Write Your Briefs

A legal brief is a written presentation of your argument. Brainstorm with the other members of your team. How does the case compare to *Gault*? Does the state of Sycamore's juvenile justice system comply with the due process requirements of *Gault* and, in particular, the right to counsel? Did Judge Jurist deny due process to Violet, or did the *Gault* requirements not apply because the judge was trying to help her? Does the failure of many juvenile courts around the country to comply with *Gault* indicate that the case was a failed experiment, and that the Supreme Court should reconsider its ruling? Alternatively, should the Court use this opportunity to strengthen its decision in *Gault* and force the states to ensure that every child in juvenile court receives effective legal representation? Which arguments are strongest for your side? Which are weakest?

You may want to divide up the arguments for research and writing. If so, be sure to work as a team to put the brief together. Otherwise, your brief may have holes or read poorly.

In real life, court rules spell out what briefs must look like and contain. Here are the rules for your brief:

1. The cover page should state the case name, *In re Violet P.* It should also state whether it is the brief for the appellant or the appellee and list the names of the lawyers. (This page will not count toward the page or word limit).

2. The text of the brief should be divided into the following sections:

   A. Statement of the issue for review: What question is before the court?

   B. Statement of the case: What is the case about? How did the lower court rule?

   C. Statement of the facts: What facts are relevant or important to the case?

   D. Summary of the argument, in 150 words or less.

   E. Argument: Spell out the legal arguments that support your side. You can split this into sections with subheadings for each part. Include references to cases or authorities that support your position.

F. Conclusion: Ask the Court to rule for your client.

3. Real appeals briefs may be 30 pages long. Limit your brief to no more than five, double-spaced, typed pages, or about 1,250 words. If possible, type the brief on a computer. Otherwise, write very neatly.

4. On an agreed-upon date, each team gives the other side a copy of its brief. Each judge receives a copy, too. If you do this in class, give the teacher a copy. Make sure each team member receives a copy, too.

Real lawyers often prepare reply briefs, in which they answer points made by the other side. You will not write a reply brief, but you should be ready to respond to the other team's points in oral argument.

Part 4: Prepare for Oral Argument
Before the oral argument, judges and law clerks should read all the briefs. They should also prepare questions for the lawyers.

Each side will have up to fifteen minutes to argue its case. Lawyers on each team may divide their time and their points among speakers. Practice your arguments together.

Step 3: Hold the Oral Argument

If possible, the room in which the argument is held should be large enough for your whole group.

Part 1: Assemble the Participants

◇ The justices sit together in the front of the room. This is the bench. They should not enter until the bailiff calls the Court to order. A speaking podium or lectern faces the bench.

◇ The appellant's team of attorneys sits at a table on one side, facing the judges.

◇ The appellee's team sits on the opposite side, also facing the judges.

◇ The reporters sit at the back.

◇ As the justices enter the room, the bailiff calls the Court to order: "Oyez (oy-yay)! Oyez! Oyez! The Supreme Court of the United States is now in session with Honorable Chief Justice _____ pre-siding. All will stand and remain standing until the justices are seated and the Chief Justice has asked all present to be seated." ("Oyez" means "Hear ye.")

Part 2: Present the Case

◇ The Chief Justice calls the case and asks if the parties are ready. A lawyer for each team answers "Yes."

◇ The appellant's first attorney approaches the podium, saying, "May it please the Court." Then the argument begins. When the appellant's attorneys finish their argument, the appellee's attorneys begin.

◇ Judges often interrupt oral argument to ask questions. Do not let this fluster you.

Answer the question carefully and honestly, and then return to your argument.

◇ Each team has up to fifteen minutes to present its argument. If the appellant's team wants to, it can save five minutes of time to rebut the appellee's argument at the end. If you do this, tell the judges and stop the argument after ten minutes.

◇ The bailiff should keep track of the time and give a two-minute warning to each team. After the arguments, the bailiff tells everyone to rise as the justices leave to debate their decision.

◇ At this time, reporters may interview lawyers for the parties and begin working on their articles.

Step 4: Publish and Report the Decision

After oral argument, the judges must decide who won the case. A majority of the judges must agree on the outcome. If students act as the judges, they should write an opinion explaining their decision. If one judge disagreed, that person can write a dissent.

The total length of all the opinions should be less than five double-spaced typed pages. (Real opinions are often much longer, as *Gault* shows.) Copies of the opinions should go to lawyers for both sides, and to the teacher.

If guest lawyers act as judges, they do not have to write opinions. They will, however, announce their decision orally. Ask them to tell your group what points persuaded them. They can also award certificates to teams for best brief and best oral argument.

Reporters may interview the lawyers again, if they wish. Reporters' stories discussing the case and the outcome are due the next day. Limit articles to five hundred words or less.

Questions for Discussion

1. Imagine that you and your friend are "hanging out" on a Saturday morning. Together, you walk past your school. To your surprise, your friend notices an open door and says, "Look, the band room is open. Let's go look around." Although there are signs all over the building warning students not to be in the building when school is not in session, and although you are aware that the consequences of breaking this rule are severe, you follow your friend inside. Your friend picks up a set of drumsticks and starts pounding on the kettle drums. Halfheartedly, you tap on a cymbal.

   You are not aware that a custodian is in the building. He hears the noise and immediately calls the police. Several minutes later, as your friend is inspecting a trombone, the door bursts open and two police officers rush in. "Hands up!" they shout. Trembling, you drop the drumsticks. Five minutes later, you find yourself in a police car, driving toward the local police station.

   a. In light of the United States Supreme Court's decision in the *Gault* case, what can the police do at this point? Can they question you and your friend about how you came to be in the band room or what you intended to do inside the school? Do you have to answer those questions? Why or why not?

b. Is there anything that the police have to tell you before they ask you questions?

2. After you arrive at the police station, a police officer places you in a small room with a table and two chairs. She leaves you there for over one hour to ponder your fate. She then returns and tells you that your parents have arrived to take you home. She further states that the police are going to charge you with juvenile delinquency and that you have to go to the county Family Court two days later.

a. Have you received adequate notice of the charges against you? Why or why not? What else (if anything) should you have been told? What other questions might you and your parents have? Is this type of oral notice sufficient?

3. When you and your parents go to the Family Court two days later, you wait for several hours and then are called into a small courtroom. The judge is seated at a large desk at the front of the room. Also present are a probation officer and the prosecutor. The judge tells you that, although you could have a lawyer represent you, many young people in your position choose not to have

one. The proceedings will be more relaxed, the judge states, if there is not a defense lawyer involved.

    a.   Why might you wish to have a lawyer defend you? What are the benefits of legal representation? What are some of the things a lawyer might do on your behalf?

    b.   Consider the judge's statement that the case would be less formal without a defense lawyer. Would this be beneficial to you? Why or why not?

    c.   In these circumstances, would you ask for a lawyer or choose not to have one? Why?

4.   The judge then tells you that you have been charged with breaking and entering and with criminal trespass. You are given a piece of paper, called a petition, that contains these charges and states that the Family Court will decide whether you should be adjudicated a juvenile delinquent. The judge also tells you that you have a right to a trial on the charges.

    a.   At such a trial, who would be responsible for proving the case against you? How much proof would be necessary under the *Winship* case?

    b.   Who might testify against you? Could the judge simply read the petition, or must witnesses be called? Which of the constitutional rights recognized by the Supreme Court in the *Gault* case is at stake here?

c.   If the prosecutor calls a witness to testify, what can, or should, your lawyer do? Which of the rights recognized by the Supreme Court in the *Gault* case is involved at this point?

d.   If the judge finds you guilty, how might you be able to challenge the decision?

Chapter Notes

Chapter 1. The Telephone Call

1. Christopher P. Manfredi, *The Supreme Court and Juvenile Justice* (Lawrence: University of Kansas Press, 1998), pp. 80–81.

2. *In re Gault*, 387 U.S. 1 (1967), p. 6.

3. Ibid.

4. Ibid., p. 7.

5. Ibid.

6. Ibid.

7. Robert Shepard, "Still Seeking the Promise of Gault: Juveniles and the Right to Counsel," *Criminal Justice*, Summer 2003, p. 24.

8. Manfredi, p. 86.

Chapter 2. "A Kind and Just Parent": The History of the Children's Court

1. *In re Gault*, 387 U.S. 1, 14-22 (1967).

2. Christopher P. Manfredi, *The Supreme Court and Juvenile Justice* (Lawrence: University of Kansas Press, 1998), pp. 29–30.

3. Julian Mack, "The Juvenile Court," 23 Harvard L. Rev. 104, 119–120 (1909).

4. Manfredi, *supra* note ii, at 208, fn. 17.

5. *In re Gault*, 387 U.S. 1, 87 S.Ct. at 1443 (1967); Manfredi, *supra* note ii, at 29, quoting the Uniform Juvenile Court Act (1968).

6. Manfredi, *supra* note ii, at p. 35.

Chapter 3. The Supreme Court and Due Process of Law

1. *Mapp* v. *Ohio*, 367 U.S. 643 (1961).

2. *Gideon* v. *Wainwright*, 372 U.S. 335 (1963).

3. *Pointer* v. *Texas*, 380 U.S. 440 (1965).

4. *Malloy* v. *Hogan*, 378 U.S. 1 (1964).

5. *Miranda* v. *Arizona*, 384 U.S. 436 (1966).

6. *Kent* v. *United States*, 383 U.S. 541 (1966).

7. Ibid. at 556.

Chapter 4. Beyond Globe: *In re Gault*'s Path to the Supreme Court

1. Christopher P. Manfredi, *The Supreme Court and Juvenile Justice* (Lawrence: University of Kansas Press, 1998), p. 87.

2. *Application of Paul L. Gault and Marjorie Gault*, 407 P.2d 760, 762 (1965).

3. Ibid.

4. Ibid.

5. *In re Gault*, 367 U.S. 1, 9 (1967).

6. Manfredi, pp. 90–91.

7. *Arizona State Department of Public Welfare* v. *Barlow*, 296 P.2d. 298 (AZ Sup. Ct. 1956).

8. Manfredi, p. 91.

9. *Application of Paul L. Gault and Marjorie Gault*, 407 P.2d at 768–770.

10. *Application of Gault*, 407 P.2d 760, 766 (Ariz. Sup. Ct. 1965).

Chapter 5. Due Process for Juveniles: The Case for Gerald Gault

1. Telephone interview with Norman Dorsen, May 12, 2005.

2. Ibid.

3. Ibid.

4. Ibid.

5. Ibid.

6. Ibid.

7. Christopher P. Manfredi, *The Supreme Court and Juvenile Justice* (Lawrence: University of Kansas Press, 1998), p. 98.

8. Ibid., pp. 98–99.

9. Telephone interview with Norman Dorsen, May 12, 2005.

10. *In re Gault*, Appellant's Brief, reprinted in B. James George, *Gault and the Juvenile Court Revolution* (Ann Arbor: Institute of Continuing Legal Education, 1968), (hereinafter "Appellant's Brief"), p. 8.

11. Ibid., p. 17.

12. Ibid., p. 18.

13. Appellant's Brief, p. 22.

14. *In re Contreras*, 109 Cal. App. 2d 787, 789, 241 P.2d 631,633 (1952), quoted in Appellant's Brief, p. 24.

15. Ibid., p. 24.

16. *Powell* v. *Alabama*, 287 U.S. 45 (1932).

17. *Gideon* v. *Wainwright*, 372 U.S. 335 (1965).

18. *Kent* v. *United States*, 383 U.S. 541 (1966).

19. *Miranda* v. *Arizona*, 384 U.S. 436 (1966).

20. 5 Wigmore on Evidence, sec. 1367, pp. 28–29 (3d ed. 1940), quoted in Appellant's Brief, p. 45.

21. *Pointer v. Texas*, 380 U.S. 400 (1965).

22. Appellant's Brief, p. 45.

23. Arizona Constitution, Article 6, sec. 15; Ariz. Rev. Stats. secs. 8-202, 8-228.

24. Appellant's Brief, p. 56.

25. Appellant's Brief, pp. 58–60.

26. Telephone interview with Norman Dorsen, May 12, 2005.

Chapter 6. **Preserving *Parens Patriae*: The Case for Arizona**

1. Christopher Manfredi, *The Supreme Court and Juvenile Justice* (Lawrence: University Press of Kansas, 1998), p. 112.

2. *In re Gault*, Brief for Appellee State of Arizona, sec. I(A), reprinted in B. James George, Jr., *Gault and the Juvenile Court Revolution* (Ann Arbor: Institute for Continuing Legal Education, 1968), (hereinafter "Appellee's Brief"), p.12.

3. Appellee's Brief, sec. I(B), quoting *In re Holmes*, 379 Pa. 599, 109 A.2d 523, p. 525, (1954), *cert. denied* 348 U.S. 973 (1955), pp. 16–17.

4. Appellee's Brief, sec. II(D), quoting Alexander, *Constitutional Rights in Juvenile Court*, 46 A.B.A. Journal 1206, 1209 (1960), p. 28.

5. *Miranda v. Arizona*, 384 U.S. 436 (1966).

Chapter 7. **Oral Argument**

1. Anthony Lewis, *Gideon's Trumpet* (New York: Vintage Books, 1966), pp. 50–51.

2. Tape of oral argument in *In re Gault*, available at <http://www.oyez.org/oyez/resource/case/181/audio resources>.

3. Ibid.

4. Ibid., and telephone interview with Norman Dorsen, May 12, 2005.

5. Tape of oral argument.

6. Ibid.

7. Ibid.

8. Ibid.

9. Ibid.

Chapter 8. No "Kangaroo Court": The Supreme Court Speaks

1. *In re Gault*, 387 U.S. 1, 18-19 (1967).

2. Ibid., p. 28.

3. *Gallegos v. Colorado*, 370 U.S. 49 (1962).

4. *In re Gault*, p. 56.

5. Ibid., p. 78 (Stewart, J., dissenting).

6. Ibid., p. 80, citing *State v. Guild*, 5 Halst. 163, 18 Am. Dec. 404 (N.J. Sup. Court).

Chapter 9. The Juvenile Court After *Gault*

1. Christopher Manfredi, *The Supreme Court and Juvenile Justice* (Lawrence: University Press of Kansas, 1998), p. 157.

2. Barry C. Feld, "*In re Gault* Revisited: A Cross-State Comparison of the Right to Counsel in Juvenile Court," 34 Crime and Delinq. 443, 458 (1988).

3. Ibid.

4. Juvenile Justice and Delinquency Prevention Act

of 1974, Pub.L. 93-415, 88 Stat. 1141 (codified in sections 5, 18, and 42 U.S.C.), quoted in American Bar Association et al., "A Call for Justice: An Assessment of Access to Counsel and Quality of Representation in Delinquency Proceedings" (1996), p. 20.

5. Ibid.

6. See generally American Bar Association et al.

7. P. Puritz and W. Shang, "Juvenile Indigent Defense: Crisis and Solutions," *Criminal Justice*, Spring 2000, p. 23.

8. American Bar Association et al.

9. See www.njdc.info.

10. *Commonwealth* v. *Webster*, 59 Mass. (5 Cush.) 295, 320 (1850), quoted in Bryan A. Garner, ed., *Black's Law Dictionary*, 8th ed. (St. Paul, MN: Thomson West, 2004), p. 1294.

11. *In re Winship*, 397 U.S. 358 (1970).

12. Ibid.; see also Manfredi, pp. 144–150.

13. *McKeiver* v. *Pennsylvania*, 403 U.S. 528 (1971).

14. *Schall* v. *Martin*, 467 U.S. 253 (1984).

15. *Roper* v. *Simmons*, 543 U.S. 551 (2005).

16. Jolanta Juszkiewicz, *Youth Crime/Adult Time: Is Justice Served?* n.d., <http:www.buildingblocksfor youth.org/ycat> (May 8, 2006).

17. Juvenile Justice and Delinquency Prevention Act of 1974, *supra* n. iv.

18. "Second Chances: Giving Kids a Chance to Make a Better Choice," *Juvenile Justice Bulletin*, May 2000, <http://www.ncjrs.org/html/ojjdp/2000_5_1/ contents.html> (May 8, 2006).

Chapter 10. Moot Court: Your Turn to Debate

1. Adapted from Millie Aulbur, "Constitutional Issues and Teenagers," The Missouri Bar, n.d., <http://www.senate.state.mo/02info/members/d07/const1.pdf> (December 10, 2004); Street Law, Inc. and The Supreme Court Historical Society, "Moot Court Activity," 2002, <http://www.landmarkcases.org/mootcourt.html> (December 10, 2004), with suggestions from Ron Fridell and Kathiann M. Kowalski.

Glossary

adjudication—A decision or judgment by a court. In the juvenile court context, an "adjudication" is a determination that a young person committed an act of juvenile delinquency.

American Civil Liberties Union (ACLU)—A national legal advocacy organization devoted to protecting civil rights and civil liberties.

confrontation, right of—The right to challenge witnesses to a criminal or delinquent act in open court. The right of confrontation is guaranteed by the Sixth and Fourteenth Amendments of the United States Constitution.

counsel, right to—The right of people charged with criminal or delinquent activity to have a lawyer represent them. The right to counsel is guaranteed by the Sixth and Fourteenth Amendments of the United States Constitution.

cross-examination—The process of questioning witnesses called by the opposing side in a legal case. The goal of cross-examination is to uncover or highlight inconsistencies, uncertainty, or untruthfulness in the witness's testimony. Like the right of confrontation and the right to counsel, the right to cross-examination is guaranteed to people charged with criminal or delinquent activity by the Sixth and Fourteenth Amendments of the United States Constitution.

detention—A facility, often resembling a jail, in which young people are held while their juvenile delinquency cases are being decided by a court.

disposition—The stage of a juvenile delinquency case in which the court decides how to respond to the young person's wrongdoing. Possible dispositions include, among others, probation, community service, placement in foster care, or a term in a state training school or other institution.

due process—The requirement, embodied in the Fifth and Fourteenth Amendments of the United State Constitution, that the three branches of government treat people according to regular, established procedures and principles and that laws do not unfairly or unreasonably affect any particular person or group of people.

family court (juvenile court)—A court that has the power to decide cases involving children and families, including juvenile delinquency matters.

juvenile—A young person, generally under the age of eighteen.

juvenile delinquency—Violations of the law committed by young people and falling within the powers of the juvenile court.

self-incrimination, privilege against—The right of

a person who is in custody or charged with a crime not to be forced to speak to the police or other government officials or testify in court. The privilege is contained in the Fifth Amendment of the United States Constitution.

transcript—A typed, word-for-word record of a court proceeding.

waiver—The transfer of a juvenile who is charged with serious or repeated violations of the law to the adult criminal justice system for prosecution.

Further Reading

Books

Bianchi, Anne. *Understanding the Law: A Teen Guide to Family Court and Minors' Rights*. New York: Rosen Publishing Group, 2000.

Ferro, Jeffrey. *Juvenile Crime*. New York: Facts on File, 2003.

Freedman, Russell. *In Defense of Liberty: The Story of America's Bill of Rights*. New York: Holiday House, 2003.

Hibbert, Adam. *Children's Rights*. North Mankato, Minn.: Sea-to-Sea Publications, 2005.

Hinds, Maurene. *You Have the Right to Know Your Rights: What Teens Should Know*. Berkeley Heights, N.J.: Enslow Publishers, Inc., 2005.

Jacobs, Thomas A. *Teens on Trial: Young People Who Challenged the Law—and Changed Your Life*. Minneapolis, Minn.: Free Spirit Publishing, 2000.

Internet Addresses

Building Blocks for Youth
<http://www.buildingblocksforyouth.org.>

"How to Conduct a Moot Court," The Missouri Bar Web site
<http://www.mobar.org/>

National Juvenile Defender Center
<http://www.njdc.info>

Index